Praise for *Everyday Encounters*

In this book, Hans Gustafson invites the reader to join him on a road trip through the landscapes of dialogue thinkers and philosophers from various contexts. The goal of the trip is to explore how to humanize our communication through dialogue, and how to build practical resilience against polarization and dehumanization. The book is full of insights and comes highly recommended!

—Anne Hege Grung, professor of interreligious studies, Faculty of Theology, University of Oslo

Everyday Encounters is a deeply thoughtful but also profoundly practical guide to dialogue. Drawing on the wisdom of dozens of leading thinkers and practitioners, Gustafson outlines a compelling vision for dialogue and its potential for transforming personal and societal relationships. This book is a vital resource for those seeking to build bridges and advance understanding and compassion across differences.

—David M. Krueger, executive director, the Dialogue Institute at Temple University

Everyday Encounters is an insightful guide that navigates the complexities of human interaction. I especially appreciated the practical wisdom for transforming discord into meaningful dialogue across diverse cultural and ideological landscapes. It's a compelling resource for anyone seeking to foster constructive connections and navigate everyday encounters with authenticity and empathy.

—Zeyneb Sayilgan, Muslim Scholar, Institute for Islamic, Christian and Jewish Studies (ICJS), Baltimore

This timely book highlights the most important skills and attitudes for making dialogue work across a spectrum of approaches. It will be particularly useful for those preparing to facilitate or participate in difficult dialogues, but anyone who wants to engage in more meaningful conversation will find helpful strategies for opening the "space between" that enables us to speak constructively across polarized divisions.

—Kevin Minister, professor of religion and director of Shenandoah Conversation, Shenandoah University; and academic associate, Essential Partners

Everyday Encounters is succinct in its presentation while deeply insightful in its content. Hans Gustafson synthesizes the works of numerous academics and practitioners, resulting in a thoughtful, practical guide to the nature and practice of dialogue. This slim volume will be a welcome resource for both the scholar of interreligious studies and the practitioner of interfaith relationships.

—Matthew Maruggi, associate professor of religion, Augsburg University

Everyday Encounters is a great introduction to dialogue as a concept and what tools and skills you need to practice dialogue. The book reminds us of the importance of seeing each other and making room for humanity. In a time of polarization, disagreement is not dangerous; dehumanization is.

—Tonje Kristoffersen, managing director, Church Dialogue Centre of Oslo

Everyday Encounters illustrates the necessity of understanding "dialogue" in the broader context of "encounter" when considering both interreligious study and practice. Hans Gustafson opens up the importance of what it means to "engage with" and humanize "the other" in person-to-person interaction, using the best of what theology, religious studies, peace and reconciliation work, and improv comedy can teach us. This is a practical and informative book for anyone looking to connect more deeply with others, personally and/or professionally, in our increasingly isolated and divided world.

—Jen Kilps, Network Executive,
Minnesota Multifaith Network

Everyday Encounters is an enlightening and accessible guide that invites us to build bridges with humanizing dialogue. Dr. Gustafson's research and practical examples are diverse and inclusive, offering insightful tools to communicate in the spirit of connection and understanding. *Everyday Encounters* inspires the practice of empathy through transformative dialogue.

—Megan Michelle, social justice scholar
and mindfulness teacher

May everyone take the principles in this book to heart and apply them. Gustafson's book lays the groundwork for the restorative change the world desperately needs.

—Marshall Bolin, conflict resolution
speaker and coach

Everyday Encounters

Everyday ENCOUNTERS

Humanizing Dialogue in Theory and Practice

Hans Gustafson

FORTRESS PRESS
MINNEAPOLIS

EVERYDAY ENCOUNTERS
Humanizing Dialogue in Theory and Practice

30 29 28 27 26 25 24   1 2 3 4 5 6 7 8 9

Library of Congress Cataloging-in-Publication Data

Names: Gustafson, Hans, author.
Title: Everyday encounters : humanizing dialogue in theory and practice / Hans Gustafson.
Description: Minneapolis : Fortress Press, [2025] | Includes bibliographical references and index. Identifiers: LCCN 2024024034 (print) | LCCN 2024024035 (ebook) | ISBN 9798889832393 (print) | ISBN 9798889832409 (ebook)
Subjects: LCSH: Interpersonal relations—Religious aspects. | Dialogue—Religious aspects. | Religions—Relations.
Classification: LCC BL626.33 .G87 2025 (print) | LCC BL626.33 (ebook) | DDC 158.2—dc23/eng/20240706
LC record available at https://lccn.loc.gov/2024024034
LC ebook record available at https://lccn.loc.gov/2024024035

Cover image: Willy Gorissen, Portrait of a girl with bow in her hair, between 1960 and 1970, sourced from Wikimedia Commons (https://tinyurl.com/Gorissen)
Cover design: Brice Hemmer

Print ISBN: 979-8-8898-3239-3
eBook ISBN: 979-8-8898-3240-9

Contents

Preface

Dialogue skills do not come naturally to me. Most, if not all, of the theories and practices in this book are neither intuitive nor instinctual for me. However, when the COVID-19 pandemic engulfed the world—soon followed by the so-called 2020 "Summer of Racial Reckoning" in the United States, marked by increased levels of isolation, political polarization, shouting across divides, discord, dehumanization, and alienation—I felt compelled to seek the best practices and wisdom from expert practitioners, theorists, and scholars of dialogue to glean some time-tested insights for human connection with others. At the time, I was writing a book on interreligious studies, now published under the title *Everyday Wisdom*. What could be more useful for *everyday wisdom* than practical dialogue skills, especially for connecting across religious differences? My original plan was to write a short chapter on dialogue for that book. However, with the help of others, I soon realized that the chapter on dialogue, which was initially very long and grew into two extensive chapters, was too important to be just a part of another book. It deserved a book of its own. This is that book.

It was a transformative experience for me, both personally and professionally, to research and write this book. It challenged me to become more human and to see the humanity in those around me. Although I am the "author" of this book, the wisdom contained herein is not mine; it is a selection of collected wisdom from others. Therefore, this is a book I will return to time and again to remind myself of the insights from experts in human communication and dialogue. I cannot imagine a context in which these skills are not relevant and important.

CHAPTER ONE

The Necessity of Dialogue

Encounters between individuals and among groups with diverse worldviews and ways of life take place in a variety of contexts and places. These encounters can be neutral, benign, constructive, and destructive. It is common for those involved to be inadequately prepared to navigate such encounters. Furthermore, sometimes such encounters may go unnoticed, which is to say encounters across difference happen constantly, and they cannot be reduced to formal oral conversations between two or more people. This chapter states the goals of the book, who it is for, and why it was written. This chapter also sets the context for thinking about dialogue as opening the "space between"; it also addresses the goals and the role of facilitation for dialogue.

GOALS OF DIALOGUE

Although there is no universal consensus on the goals and aims of dialogue, some general goals can be identified. For peace studies scholar Lisa Schirch and dialogue studies scholar David Campt, "The primary goal of dialogue is to help participants gain greater insight into their own perspectives, values, patterns of thinking, and biases."[1] According to the Karuna Center for Peacebuilding, an American organization that

---

1 Lisa Schirch and David Campt, *The Little Book of Dialogue for Difficult Subjects: A Practical, Hands-On Guide* (Intercourse, PA: Good Books, 2007), 15.

fosters sustainable peace by empowering divided communities to achieve mutual understanding, reconcile differences, and strengthen resilience through long-term partnerships in conflict-affected areas, "The main objective of dialogue is to strengthen relationships through mutual and deep understanding of motivations, interests and communication styles of all participants."[2] These foundational perspectives show that the scope of dialogue extends beyond mere conversation and holds a transformative potential. According to the Nansen Center for Peace and Dialogue, a globally recognized knowledge center in Lillehammer, Norway, and meeting point for dialogue and conflict transformation, "Dialogue work is about reaching deeper levels of understanding."[3] And for the International

---

2 Karuna Center for Peacebuilding, *Community Dialogue Handbook*, ed. Joanne Lauterjung (Amherst, MA: Karuna Center for Peacebuilding, 2018), 3.

3 Norunn Grande and Christiane Seehausen, eds., *The Nansen Handbook for Trainers in Dialogue and Conflict Transformation* (Lillehammer: Nansen Freds-senter, 2018), 7.

Dialogue Centre (KAICIID), an intergovernmental organization fostering dialogue among religious leaders and policymakers globally, "The aim of dialogue is to overcome misunderstandings and dispel stereotypes so as to increase mutual understanding."[4] This emphasis on developing deeper understanding and dispelling stereotypes, as highlighted by leading organizations, sets the stage for exploring the many possible aims of dialogue.

The aim of dialogue is not agreement or consensus, nor is it to get everyone on the same page. Rather, the goal most often includes the simple task to listen, learn, and understand. Above all, dialogue is about listening. Dialogue in the context of interreligious relations, a context with deep ideological and practical differences, helps robustly unveil its significance as a tool for fostering mutual understanding. It highlights

---

4 Mohamed Abu-Nimer, Anas Alabbadi, and Cynthia Marquez, *Building Bridges* (Kuala Lumpur: World Organization of the Scout Movement; Vienna: International Dialogue Centre, 2018), 20.

transferable principles applicable to several other contexts. Jennifer Lewis of the Lutheran World Federation observes, "Ultimately, the possible goals of interreligious dialogue come in as many colors as the communities participating, and every community's unique context and theological vision will guide it to a different understanding of the dialogue's purpose."[5] To broaden matters more, the Council for Religions and Life Stance Communities in Norway (STL), a Norwegian umbrella organization aimed at ensuring equality and fostering dialogue among diverse religious and life stance communities, recognizes that "not every dialogue needs to have a

---

5 Jennifer Lewis, *Embarking on the Journey of Interreligious Dialogue* (Geneva: The Lutheran World Federation, 2015), 19. The Karuna Center for Peacebuilding recognizes that "other common goals of dialogue may include: share information; establish relationships and trust; identify and clarify issues and shared values; share perspectives, histories, beliefs and opinions in a safe and constructive environment; develop ideas and options; and/or develop recommendations" (Karuna Center for Peacebuilding's *Community Dialogue Handbook*, 4).

goal beyond the conversation itself, but many dialogues do. . . . Whatever the goal or task of the dialogue, it is important for us to approach this aspect of the dialogue by being clear about our own objectives, and by being ready to listen to the objectives of others."[6] Just as organizations provide diverse perspectives on the goals of dialogue, the complexity of dialogue also surfaces in the experiences and insights of individual communities and practitioners.

Some individuals and communities have more specific aims for interreligious dialogue, such as Pope Francis. Drawing on the Catholic bishops of India, Pope Francis explains, "Dialogue between the followers of different religions does not take place simply for the sake of diplomacy, consideration or tolerance. In the words of the Bishops of India, 'the goal of dialogue is to establish friendship, peace and

---

6 Helge Svare, in cooperation with the Council for Religious and Life Stance Communities, "Explanation of the Dialogue Poster," the Council for Religious and Life Stance Communities, Oslo, 2017, 2.

harmony, and to share the spiritual and moral values and experiences in the spirit of truth and love.'"[7] This emphasis on friendship, peace, and the sharing of values underscores the profound and specific objectives that can drive interreligious dialogue and reflects its potential to foster deeper understanding and unity among diverse faith communities.

Not all share the same goal(s) of dialogue. Scholar of religion Jennifer Fields asks whether the goal of friendship in interreligious dialogue is shared by all. Fields observes that although the concept of friendship in interreligious dialogue is often taken for granted as a universal goal, it is perceived and valued differently across religious traditions. For instance, Fields's research argues that while Christians *generally* tend to

---

7 Pope Francis, *Fratelli Tutti* (Vatican: Libreria Editrice Vaticana, 2020), 271; citing the Catholic Bishops' Conference of India, "Response of the Church in India to the Present-day Challenges," March 9, 2016, https://www.vatican.va/content/francesco/en/encyclicals/documents/papa-francesco_20201003_enciclica-fratelli-tutti.html#_ftn259.

view friendship as an inherent and unproblematic outcome of interfaith engagements, Muslims *generally* more often approach the idea of interfaith friendship more sparingly.[8] Scholar of religion and interfaith dialogue pioneer Leonard Swidler states it simply: "The general goal of dialogue (of the Head) is for each side to learn, and to change accordingly."[9] The pivotal claim here is the importance of being open to the possibility of change, which is a common reoccurring theme among dialogue practitioners and commentators.

Schirch and Campt frequently point to dialogue as a potential space for self-reflection, which "can lead to other changes."[10] Likewise, dialogue can also be "a method for social

8 Jennifer R. Fields, "Questioning the Promotion of Friendship in Interfaith Dialogue: Interfaith Friendship in Light of the Emphasis on Particularity in Scriptural Reasoning" (PhD diss., University of Cambridge, 2020), https://doi.org/10.17863/CAM.51377.

9 Leonard Swidler, *Dialogue for Interreligious Understanding* (New York: Palgrave Macmillan, 2014), 26.

10 Schirch and Campt, *The Little Book of Dialogue*, 15.

change. . . . The goal of dialogue is to create greater understanding, which in turn may motivate participants to take action personally or collectively with others."[11] Change involves not just intra- or interpersonal transformation, although that is an admirable aim and outcome; dialogue can also, ideally, create "a space for people to build relationships and develop new networks that increase people's vision and desire to take collective action."[12] However, as prominent Norwegian peace scholar and practitioner Steinar Bryn and others at the Nansen Center are careful to point out, "The purpose of dialogue is not to force or allure others into changing. That is the way propaganda operates. It often has the opposite effect when values are tried to be forced on a person from the outside. . . . Dialogue knows no other coercion than what lies in the essence of dialogue itself; it consists of listening, learning, and perhaps being changed

11 Schirch and Campt, *The Little Book of Dialogue*, 65.
12 Schirch and Campt, *The Little Book of Dialogue*, 70.

oneself."[13] In this sense, a fundamental aim of dialogue is to foster mutual respect and understanding rather than attempting to persuade, convert, or necessarily win over others.

David Bohm, a prominent twentieth-century physicist known for his innovative work in quantum theory and his influential contributions to the philosophy of dialogue and communication, creatively states the overarching attitude of dialogue as that which makes "possible a flow of meaning in the whole group, out of which may emerge a new understanding. It's something new, which may not have been in the starting point at all. It's something creative. And this shared meaning is the 'glue' or 'cement' that holds people and societies together."[14] Building on Bohm's

13 Steinar Bryn, Inge Edisvåg, and Ingunn Skurdall, *Understanding the Other: Dialogue as a Tool and an Attitude to Life* (Lillehammer: Nansen Fredssenter, 2015), 17.

14 David Bohm, *On Dialogue* (London: Routledge, 2014), 33; cited in Frances Sleap and Omer Sener, *Dialogue Theories*, ed. Paul Weller (London: Dialogue Society, 2013), 41.

insight into the creative emergence of shared meaning, the next section reflects on dialogue facilitation, which can be crucial for generating collective understanding and coherence.

DIALOGUE FACILITATION

Although dialogue can happen without a facilitator and at any time, having a facilitator is often helpful and sometimes necessary. Schirch and Campt claim, "The role of the facilitator may be the most important element of dialogue,"[15] while the International Dialogue Centre argues, "An essential element or actor in the dialogue is the facilitator."[16] This section addresses dialogue facilitation by reflecting on the role of the facilitator, as well as the benefits and limitations of having one.

The verb *facilitate* derives from the Latin root *facilis*, which gave rise to the English *facile*,

15 Schirch and Campt, *The Little Book of Dialogue*, 58.
16 Abu-Nimer et al., *Building Bridges*, 66.

meaning "to make easy or to render less difficult." Hence, the role of the facilitator is to make the process of dialogue less difficult for all participants. "To make easy" does not mean to make comfortable and luxurious. Rather, the facilitator operates as a neutral mediator (to the extent that neutrality[17] is possible) who enables, as influential twentieth-century Brazilian educator and critical pedagogue Paulo Freire taught, "all voices to be heard without pressuring individuals into speaking."[18] Facilitation involves creating a conducive environment where open communication is encouraged. This role is not just about alleviating difficulties but also about actively guiding the dialogue, ensuring it remains productive and inclusive. By managing

17 The Karuna Center for Peacebuilding identities the top facilitation skill of "neutrality—the ability to see all sides of a situation and support everyone to be heard, regardless of their opinion" (*Community Dialogue Handbook*, 13).

18 Michael Atkinson, "Paulo Freire," in *Dialogue Theories*, vol. 2, ed. Omer Sener, Frances Sleap, and Paul Weller (London: Dialogue Society, 2016), 127.

the dynamics of the conversation, the facilitator helps navigate through complex or challenging topics, thereby making the process of dialogue smoother and more effective for all participants.

Austrian-born Jewish philosopher of dialogue Martin Buber observes that "undoubtedly the most important conditions that facilitators might strive to put in place are internal to themselves. . . . personal qualities are vital. The openness and presence of one person will often inspire the same in another."[19] Becoming a skilled facilitator need not be a matter of being born with the innate qualities conducive to easing the dialogue process, but rather, as Buber recognized, these qualities can be learned and developed. A person develops the facilitation "qualities of personal unity, presence and openness," according to Buber, "by repeatedly risking encounter. In exposing oneself to interpersonal contact and learning to let one's guard down one can become more oriented towards the I-You

19 Sleap and Sener, *Dialogue Theories*, 60.

world. Experience is essential for the development of quality dialogue facilitators."[20] In this manner, facilitators develop skills through direct experience and encounter.

Skilled facilitators develop several qualities that can allow them to be more accepted as neutral mediators by all participants. Several, or perhaps all, of these qualities are not unique to dialogue facilitation but stand out as useful transferrable leadership skills to be leveraged in various contexts. Two skills in particular are especially relevant for facilitating dialogue across difference: personal awareness and authenticity. *Personal awareness* gets at the core of cultivating leadership. In the context of dialogue, it means the facilitator is not only "aware of his/her own biases and perceptions, but also of how he/she is perceived."[21] *Authenticity* means the facilitator needs to "'walk the talk' and be natural about what he/she believes. This does not mean sharing

---

20 Sleap and Sener, *Dialogue Theories*, 61.
21 Abu-Nimer et al., *Building Bridges*, 67.

his/her opinion on the subject matter, but rather believing in the process and the potential of the process."[22]

The facilitator does not need to be an expert on the topic or subject under discussion. Mohammed Abu-Nimer, a well-known American expert on conflict resolution and transformation, points out that "in some cases, it is a blessing that the facilitator doesn't have much knowledge about the topic, because some would argue that the less he/she knows about the topic, the more natural he/she will be toward the discussions and its outcomes."[23] This may help explain why often the best interviewers tend to have very limited knowledge, expertise, or experience with many of the topics, questions, books, and fields of their interviewees. It may give the interviewer permission to ask the "dumb" or obvious questions in seemingly naïve and basic ways that force the

---

22 Abu-Nimer et al., *Building Bridges*, 67.
23 Abu-Nimer et al., *Building Bridges*, 68.

interviewee to answer in a very simple and plain language.

Hence, a neutral facilitator with little to no knowledge of the topic forces the participants to begin with basic questions and commence from as few premises as possible (e.g., as Socrates models in Plato's Dialogues). It also allows participants an opportunity to tell their stories afresh from the beginning and ground up. What's more, it opens space between the various positions and produces the "fifth province" or "third culture."

THE SPACE BETWEEN, THE FIFTH PROVINCE, AND THE THIRD CULTURE

Martin Buber is one of the best-known twentieth-century Jewish thinkers. This Austrian Jewish and Israeli intellectual proposed a rigorous philosophy of dialogue centered in human relationship. Human beings relate to each other in two basic modes: the I-It mode (*Ich-Es*) and the I-Thou (*Ich-Du*) mode, the latter of which qualifies as real dialogue, for it alone requires one to use one's whole being[24] in treating and relating to the other person as a unique whole person themselves.[25]

Buber claims, "The world as experience belongs to the basic word I-It. The basic word I-You establishes the world of relation."[26] In other words, in the I-It mode, humans experience others as an object (it) with attention to their various qualities and character (e.g., like a geologist experiencing and examining the earth). In the I-Thou mode, humans do not experience the other, but rather they *encounter* the other by standing in relation to them. Hence, experience for the individual is decentered, and the space

---

24 Martin Buber, *I and Thou*, trans. Walter Kaufman (New York: Simon and Schuster, 1970), 62.

25 Sleap and Sener, *Dialogue Theories*, 53.

26 Buber, *I and Thou*, 56.

between, or the zone of relation, becomes centered as the primary locus for genuine dialogue.[27]

Bryn and colleagues from the Nansen Center for Peace and Dialogue call attention to the legend of the so-called "fifth province" from Irish mythology, where, in the Ireland of old, the four provinces came together and met. The fifth province served as a neutral zone where conflict and disputes could be dealt with and mediated. It was not understood to be a literal geophysical space on the map; rather, it was a metaphysical space that could be summoned within any of the four provinces (as it rotated among them)

27 Oddbjørn Leirvik, contemporary Norwegian pioneer of the formal academic field of interreligious studies, draws heavily on Buber by advocating that "interreligious studies can be meaningfully done only in a willingness to reflect critically on one's own position in the space between." This points to the indispensable role of self-reflection and openness to self-implication in nurturing self-awareness in the spaces between, not only for dialogue but also for the academic study of interreligious relations. Oddbjørn Leirvik, "Interreligious Studies," in *Contested Spaces, Common Ground*, ed. Ulrich Winkler, Lidia Rodriguez, and Oddbjørn Leirvik (Leiden: Brill, 2016), 36.

when needed. In the fifth province, special rules applied that negated daily law. Weapons were laid down, clannish symbols were discarded, and the common good of all four provinces was elevated above tribal concerns. Bryn and colleagues suggest that "the dialogue space is such a fifth province,"[28] in which individuals decenter themselves and their experiences and, in a very Buberian manner, center the relations that exist between and among the I's and Thous.

Hans-Georg Gadamer might recognize this fifth province as an opportunity for individuals to transcend their preexisting horizons and discern novel insights that were previously unknown. Gadamer, a twentieth-century German philosopher, understood this dialogue process as "a fusion of horizons"[29] (*Horizontverschmelzung*)—that is, a coming together of horizons in an ongoing and never-ending fashion that discloses the

---

28 Bryn et al., *Understanding the Other*, 12.

29 Hans-Georg Gadamer, *Truth and Method*, 2nd rev. ed., trans. Joel Weinsheimer and Donald Marshall (New York: Continuum, 2003), 307.

truth.[30] Gadamer's fusion of horizons has influenced models for dialogue and intergroup conflict transformation by emphasizing a hermeneutical process of shared dialogic novel understanding. This is perhaps a complicated way to suggest that participants and groups enter into a dialogue with their preconceived "prejudices"—"the idea that we already carry around with us an understanding because of the religious and cultural tradition to which we belong"[31]; however, the dialogue process generates new meanings and insights, sometimes referred to as "a third culture."[32] The ongoing, never-ending dialectical back-and-forth dialogue process reveals, challenges,

30 Oliver Ramsbotham, "Hans-Georg Gadamer," in *Dialogue Theories*, vol. 2, ed. Omer Sener, Frances Sleap, and Paul Weller (London: Dialogue Society, 2016), 142.

31 Marianne Moyaert, "Interreligious Dialogue," in *Understanding Interreligious Relations*, ed. David Cheetham, Douglas Pratt, and David Thomas (Oxford: Oxford University Press, 2013), 207.

32 Benjamin Boome, "Managing Differences in Conflict Resolution," in *Conflict Resolution Theory and Practice*, ed. Denis Sandole and Hugo van der Merwe (Manchester: Manchester University Press, 1993), 97–111; cited in Ramsbotham, "Hans-Georg Gadamer," 145.

changes, refines, and corrects individuals' prejudices[33] and generates a third culture, or fusion of horizons.

SO WHAT?

Dialogue is an incredibly versatile tool that can be applied to virtually any situation or context. The tool has been used at various levels, ranging from individual interactions and familial discussions to larger community settings and even high-level geopolitical negotiations involving heads of state in conflict zones. Despite being used in Israel, Palestine, and Northern Ireland to navigate across religious division, dialogue is not explicitly limited to interreligious encounters. Dialogue serves as a fundamental means of communication, occupying a central position at the core of human interactions. It is crucial for healthy relationships and effective leadership, and it plays a pivotal role in fostering honesty and empathy, two foundational virtues for human flourishing.

33 Moyaert, "Interreligious Dialogue," 20.

Without the ability to communicate and engage in conversation, everything humans love and hold dear may inevitably crumble. Without proper communication and understanding, trust and connection erode, resulting in the breakdown of relationships, families, neighborhoods, teams, organizations, corporations, and ultimately entire societies and civilizations.[34] Without the ability to engage in dialogue, particularly across differences, we descend into destructive tactics such as violence and insults. In the overly binary climate of the contemporary world, there is no shortage of divisions to push people apart. Consider the US presidential elections since 2016, especially in 2020 and 2024, that have pitted people with deep ideological differences against each other. As always, after the winners and losers of the election are declared, many people are disappointed, while many others are elated. Given that most

34 Peter Boghossian, interview by Alan Campbell, "Peter Boghossian: How to Have Impossible Conversations," Watching America Podcast, October 16, 2020, https://mediaplayer.whro.org/program/watchingamerica/e/watchingamerica-friday-october-16th-2020.

Americans have friends, family, and peers who likely hold diverse political and ideological perspectives, engaging in political conversations or discussions across difference can pose challenges. Increasingly, there is an alarming trend to disassociate from family, friends, and neighbors with differing and diverse worldviews from one's own, whether the views are religious, political, ideological, or issue-specific.[35]

---

35 Countless studies and surveys point to this (e.g., Tovia Smith, "'Dude, I'm Done': When Politics Tears Families and Friendships Apart," NPR.org, October 27, 2020, heard on *All Things Considered*, https://www.npr.org/2020/10/27/928209548/dude-i-m-done-when-politics-tears-families-and-friendships-apart; Leticia Bode, "Pruning the News Feed: Unfriending and Unfollowing Political Content on Social Media," *Research and Politics* 3, no. 3 [2016]: 1–8. https://doi.org/10.1177/2053168016661873; Jeff Diaman, "One-in-Six Americans Have Taken Steps to See Less of Someone on Social Media due to Religious Content," Pew Research Center, June 21, 2023, https://www.pewresearch.org/short-reads/2023/06/21/one-in-six-americans-have-taken-steps-to-see-less-of-someone-on-social-media-due-to-religious-content/; Kory Floyd et al., "'If You Disagree, Unfriend Me Now': Exploring the Phenomenon of Invited Unfriending," *American Journal of Applied Psychology* 7, no. 1 [2019]: 20–29, https://doi.org/10.12691/ajap-7-1-3).

This book introduces readers to the *what*, *why*, and *how* of dialogue as a valuable tool to navigate encounters and conversations across difference. It invites readers to engage those around them with attentive listening and sensitivity to their needs and with an eye to responding accordingly. It serves as a resource for constructive human engagement, whether it be in community, with family members and friends, or in professional leadership roles, working with colleagues, managing employees, brokering business relationships, or serving clients and patients in health-care or legal professions. The theory and practice of dialogue are broad and fundamental—and adaptable to most contexts.

CHAPTER TWO

The Nature of Dialogue

This chapter addresses the nature and theory of dialogue, exploring its purpose and objectives. It draws insights from philosophers, theologians, practitioners, and modern institutes dedicated to peace and dialogue. The chapter then delineates six principal types of dialogue: praxis-oriented, cognitive, existential, humanizing, ambassadorial, and intrapersonal. Finally, it distinguishes dialogue from debate and other related but distinct activities.

WHAT IS DIALOGUE?

Dialogue, whether through words or unspoken understanding between two or more individuals or groups, is a fundamental expression of what it means to be human. It embodies a process of meaningful self-giving communication that fosters understanding, builds relationships, and journeys toward shared truths. Martin Buber famously stated, "All actual life is encounter."[1] A primary mode of human encounter occurs through conversation, which involves speaking and listening. In his landmark 2020 encyclical *Fratelli Tutti*, Pope Francis stated that "approaching, speaking, listening, looking at, coming to know and understand one another, and to find common ground: all these things

---

1 Martin Buber, *I and Thou*, trans. Walter Kaufman (New York: Simon and Schuster, 1970), 62.

are summed up in the one word 'dialogue.' If we want to encounter and help one another, we have to dialogue."[2] This chapter explores the expanding use and versatility of dialogue in the contemporary English-speaking world. It defines what dialogue is (and is not) and examines the various forms it can take, including different approaches and methods for engaging in it.

The term *dialogue* etymologically comes from the classical Greek *dialogos* (διάλογος) with roots in *διά* ("through") and *λογος* ("logos") to mean "reasoned thought or expression throughout, across, or between."[3] Sometimes, *dialogue* is mistakenly thought to be synonymous with *duologue*, which specifically denotes a conversation between two people. In fact, *dialogue* refers to a conversation involving two or more people. This is distinguished from *monologue*, which

---

2 Pope Francis, *Fratelli Tutti* (Vatican City: Libreria Editrice Vaticana, 2020), 198.

3 Paul Weller, "Introduction: How and Why Should We Study Dialogue?" in *Dialogue Theories*, vol. 2, ed. Omer Sener, Frances Sleap, and Paul Weller (London: Dialogue Society, 2016), 19.

is a speech by a single person.[4] *Dialogue* may be evoked as shorthand for "thinking between" through the act of speaking and listening.[5] To be sure, a plurality of definitions for *dialogue* abound, and it cannot be assumed that everyone operates with the same definition.[6]

A functional and provisional working definition from the Dialogue Society (which oversees the Institute for Dialogue Studies and the *Journal of Dialogue Studies*) articulates that dialogue "consists of meaningful interaction and exchange between people of different groups (social, cultural, political and religious) who come together through various kinds

---

4 Marianne Moyaert, "Interreligious Dialogue," in *Understanding Interreligious Relations*, ed. David Cheetham, Douglas Pratt, David Thomas (Oxford: Oxford University Press, 2013), 205.

5 Leonard Swidler, *Dialogue for Interreligious Understanding* (New York: Palgrave Macmillan, 2014), 87; Joanne Lauterjung, ed., *Community Dialogue Handbook: A Guide for Facilitating Community Engagement* (Amherst, MA: Karuna Center for Peacebuilding, 2018), 3.

6 Frances Sleap and Omer Sener, *Dialogue Theories*, ed. Paul Weller (London: Dialogue Society, 2013), 17.

of conversations or activities with a view to increased understanding."[7] Schirch and Campt's *The Little Book of Dialogue for Difficult Subjects* defines dialogue succinctly as "a communication process that aims to build relations between people as they share experiences, ideas, and information about a common concern."[8] The International Dialogue Centre (KAIICID), a partnership of Spain, Saudi Arabia, Austria, and the Vatican, defines dialogue as "a secure means of communication between individuals or groups aimed at the exchange of views, knowledge, understandings, impressions and perceptions to reach a common understanding of the subject matter at heart of a given dialogue."[9] The Nansen

---

7 "Our Approach," Dialogue Society, 2019, http://www.dialoguesociety.org/about-us.html.

8 Lisa Schirch and David Campt, *The Little Book of Dialogue for Difficult Subjects* (New York: Good Books, 2007), 6.

9 Mohammed Abu-Nimer, Anas Alabbadi, and Cynthia Marquez, *Building Bridges: Guide for Dialogue Ambassadors* (Kuala Lumpur: World Organization of Scout Movement and Vienna: The International Dialogue Centre, 2018), 20.

Center for Peace and Dialogue in Lillehammer, Norway, defines dialogue as "a conversation based on humility, respect and openness which allows us to learn about each other. By learning about each other, unmanageable situations can become manageable. Dialogue enhances relationships in a community and strengthens the social fabric. Dialogue opens the door to peaceful co-existence."[10] The Nansen Center's handbook for trainers in dialogue goes a step further by emphasizing that dialogue, as a way of communication, "focuses on understanding 'the other,' rather than trying to convince them that you are right. This understanding enables us to build sustainable relationships and can create a solid foundation for successful mediation and negotiations."[11] Textbook definitions such as these often fail to capture the nuanced essence

---

10 "Dialogue," Nansen Peace Center, accessed February 9, 2021, https://www.peace.no/dialog/.

11 Norunn Grande and Christiane Seehausen, eds., *The Nansen Handbook for Trainers in Dialogue and Conflict Transformation* (Lillehammer: Nansen Fredssenter, 2018), 8.

of dialogue, which suggests the need to explore broader and deeper visions of dialogue to fully understand its intimate core.

Beyond these initial definitions, consider the contributions of individual thinkers who have offered theoretical perspectives on dialogue, rooted in deeper, more existential meanings of dialogue often tied to what it means to be human. American quantum physicist David Bohm exemplifies a deeper vision of dialogue in his suggestion that it is "a stream of meaning flowing among and through us and between us."[12] Alfred North Whitehead, the well-known twentieth-century English philosopher, famously quipped that the "safest general characterization of the European philosophical tradition is that it consists of a series of footnotes to Plato."[13] With the concept of dialogue in the West, it may be no different. Socrates, as portrayed by

---

12 David Bohm, *On Dialogue* (London: Routledge, 2014), 7; cited in Sleap and Sener, *Dialogue Theories*, 39.

13 Alfred North Whitehead, *Process and Reality*, corrected ed., ed. David Ray Griffin and Donald W. Sherburne (New York: Free Press, 1978), 39.

Plato, modeled the Western notion of dialogue as a mutual journey of truth-seeking that two or more people embark on together. Socrates believed that truth already exists inherently in all persons and simply needs to be birthed (or, more accurately, midwifed) out through conversation and encounter with others; that is, "learning through questions and answers—through dialogue—became a means for remembering a truth that we all carry inside ourselves, but in a forgotten form."[14]

Socrates exemplified the midwifery function of asking questions to pull the truth out of his dialogue partners. Hence, unlike debate or prosecutorial questioning, dialogue is a friendly journey toward truth through speaking, listening, questioning, and reasoning (i.e., *dia-logos*). The truth lies in wait among the dialogue

---

14 Steinar Bryn, Inge Edisvåg, and Ingunn Skurdall, "What Is Dialogue?" in *Understanding the Other: Dialogue as a Tool and an Attitude to Life* (Lillehammer: Nansen Fredssenter, 2015), 10.

participants and is released through the conversation. This Socratic midwifery model of mutual truth-seeking dialogue corresponds with elicitive methodologies often employed in conflict mediation, transformation, and resolution contexts. An elicitive model,[15] as its name suggests, assumes that truth, wisdom, and resolution can be elicited (provoked, produced, or drawn) from the dialogue participants and the process itself. In practice, asset-based community development provides a concrete example of this dialogue theory in that it commences with the assumption that the participants in the community are sufficient and necessary assets (with their experience, wisdom, knowledge, gifts, talents, and resources) to be used in achieving their shared goals. The question then becomes: What are the purpose and goal(s) of dialogue?

---

15 Grande and Seehausen, eds., *The Nansen Handbook*, 65.

THE PURPOSE OF DIALOGUE

"Life by its very nature is dialogic. To live means to participate in dialogue,"[16] observes the twentieth-century Russian philosopher Mikhail Bakhtin. He suggests dialogue serves as the primary mechanism through which a person discovers their own self, to the degree that such a thing is possible. Dialogue begins at the moment of birth, or before, in a baby's dialogic encounter with its mother and continues throughout life as a person self-defines vis-à-vis dialogue with others, societal norms, culture, ideology, beliefs, and so on.[17] Paulo Freire, the influential twentieth-century Brazilian pedagogical theorist and community developer, echoes Bakhtin in support of the inherent potential of dialogue to humanize. Scholar of dialogue, Michael Atkinson argues

16 Mikhail Bakhtin, *Problems of Dostoevsky's Poetics*, trans. Caryl Emerson (Minneapolis: University of Minnesota Press, 1984), 293; cited by Jeff Shires, "Mikhail Bakhtin," in *Dialogue Theories*, vol. 2, ed. Omer Sener, Frances Sleap, and Paul Weller (London: Dialogue Society, 2016), 31.

17 Jeff Shires, "Mikhail Bakhtin," 32.

that "Freire's great legacy . . . is a recognition that to be human is to engage in dialogue, or at least have the potential to do so."[18] Martin Buber goes a step further and declares that an individual is not fully human without living with the intensity of, what he refers to as, "I-You" relationships and dialogic encounters, in which one experiences and treats the other as an equal and a friend.[19] Buber maintains the I-You encounter dispels the dehumanizing and essentializing of stereotyping and prejudice.[20] Not only does dialogue have the potential to humanize one's own self and others, it can also serve as a means toward recognizing, and perhaps realizing, common public goods.

Pope Francis, in his *Fratelli Tutti*, a 2020 encyclical letter—a formal letter on matters of doctrine sent by the pope to Catholics worldwide—emphasizes ethical relationships and social friendship as ways to build a more

---

18 Michael Atkinson, "Paulo Freire," in *Dialogue Theories*, vol. 2, ed. Omer Sener, Frances Sleap, and Paul Weller (London: Dialogue Society, 2016), 131.

19 Buber, *I and Thou*, 85.

20 Sleap and Sener, *Dialogue Theories*, 60.

just and peaceful world. Francis suggests that a "lack of dialogue means that in these individual sectors[21] people are concerned not for the common good, but for the benefits of power or, at best, for ways to impose their own ideas."[22] As Steinar Bryn and others at the Nansen Center point out, imposition of ideas is not dialogue but propaganda:

> The purpose of dialogue is not to force or allure others into changing. That is the way propaganda operates. It often has the opposite effect when values are tried to be forced on a person from the outside. "I love to be moved, I hate to be forced," T.S. Elliot once said. . . . Dialogue knows no other coercion than what lies in the essence of dialogue itself. It consists of listening, learning and perhaps being changed oneself. One cannot change

---

21 For example, governments, economics, politics, communications, religion, and other spheres.

22 Pope Francis, *Fratelli Tutti*, 202.

> another human being if one is not open to being changed by the same human being.[23]

In the same spirit, Pope Francis preaches that "in a pluralistic society, dialogue is the best way to realize what ought always be affirmed and respected apart from any ephemeral consensus."[24] Dialogue holds promise for self-discovery, understanding, mutual relation-building, and several other possible goals and outcomes. Just as no single definition of dialogue exists, no one mode of dialogue reigns supreme. Dialogue can be complex.[25] Regardless of definition, mode, or goal, dialogue can be a promising starting point, and perhaps an essential tool, for forging trusting and sustainable relationships and learning under various conditions and in multiple contexts.

---

23 Bryn et al., "What Is Dialogue?," 17.

24 Pope Francis, *Fratelli Tutti*, 211.

25 Karsten Lehmann, "Interreligious Dialogue in Context," *Interdisciplinary Journal for Religion and Transformation in Contemporary Society* 6 (2020): 240.

TYPES OF DIALOGUE

There are several helpful ways to conceptualize what sort of activity dialogue is, its proper format, goals, and how it ought to look.[26] This nebulosity can be an asset, for it demonstrates the flexible agility of dialogue to be potentially adapted and applied to various contexts and sought-out outcomes. Interreligious dialogue can be very complex with several contextual variables determining its look and feel. Key variables include the following:

- a dialogue's *participants* (Who is and is not involved? Government officials, common laypeople, religious leaders, scholars)
- its *structure* (Is it local/domestic/international? Is it small/large? Is it bi- or multilateral?)
- its *theme and goals* (What are the desired outcomes? What constitutes success? Who gets to decide?)

26 Sleap and Sener, *Dialogue Theories*, 17.

- its *intention* (Why do people attend and what motivates their engagement?)
- its *principles* (Who sets the agenda? What are the ground rules or principles for the encounter?)[27]

There is a growing supply of neatly organized typologies that distinguish various types of interreligious dialogue based on mode, outcome, and content, among other things. To enhance clarity, and with a nod toward brevity and precision, the major influential typologies are succinctly consolidated below.

As such, four major types of interreligious dialogue emerge. This typology is neither exhaustive nor perfect, and the types are not mutually exclusive to one another. No doubt, other types exist between, within, and beyond the types mentioned here. The aim here is to sketch a broad landscape of types for the purpose of capturing where contemporary thought rests

27 Drawn from Moyaert, "Interreligious Dialogue," 201; and Sergey Melnik, "Types of Interreligious Dialogue," *Journal of Interreligious Studies* 31 (2020): 54.

(so far). The four major types of dialogue are (1) praxis-oriented, (2) cognitive, (3) existential, and (4) humanizing. In addition to these four types, honorable mention can be made of (a) ambassadorial and (b) intrapersonal.

Praxis-Oriented Dialogue

Praxis-oriented dialogue is active, collaborative, and concrete. It does not prioritize, or may not even involve, literal dialogue in the colloquial sense of the word (e.g., discussion, conversation, etc.). Dialogue need not be understood as literal verbal communication or conversation between two or more people, but rather it can be understood in a much broader sense to include encounter, relations, and engagement.

The prominent American scholar known for his work in interreligious dialogue, Leonard Swidler, proposes the "Dialogue of the Hands,"[28] which seeks *the ethical good* by

---

28 Swidler, *Dialogue for Interreligious Understanding*, 17.

aiming to "make the world a better place"[29] through the coming together of people and communities who orient around religion differently to work with and alongside each other to achieve concrete positive change in the world. Although Swidler has religion in mind as the primary axis around which this mode of dialogue orients, its principles apply all the same to other contexts that involve people coming together from different (sometimes clashing) contexts to work toward goods they have in common.

Pope John Paul II (1920–2005) identified praxis-oriented dialogue as the "dialogue of deeds"[30] in 1984, and in 1991 the Vatican deemed it by its more common name today as

29 Melnik, "Types of Interreligious Dialogue," 58; Swidler, *Dialogue for Interreligious Understanding*, 17.

30 John Paul II, *The Attitude of the Church towards the Followers of Other Religions: Reflections and Orientations on Dialogue and Mission* (Vatican: Pontifical Council for Interreligious Dialogue, 1984), 31.

the "dialogue of action,"[31] in which religiously diverse groups "collaborate for the integral development and liberation of people." Predating these Roman Catholic pronouncements, Eric J. Sharpe, twentieth-century English scholar of religion and dialogue, identified this type as "secular dialogue," for it "concentrates entirely on the situation of man in the world, aiming solely at the recognition of joint concern and the need for joint secular action, irrespective of divergences in religious conviction," and thus it leverages the reality that "in practice . . . all the great religions have shown increased interest in social and political action for the amelioration of man's lot on earth."[32] This evolution in terminology and emphasis, from "dialogue

---

31 Pontifical Council for Inter-religious Dialogue, *Dialogue and Proclamation: Reflection and Orientations on Interreligious Dialogue and the Proclamation of the Gospel of Jesus Christ* (Vatican: Pontifical Council for Interreligious Dialogue, 1991), 42.

32 Eric J. Sharpe, "The Goals of Inter-Religious Dialogue," in *Truth and Dialogue in World Religions*, ed. John Hick (Philadelphia: Westminster Press, 1974), 85.

of deeds" to "dialogue of action" and Sharpe's "secular dialogue," reflects a growing awareness and commitment across religious traditions to collaborate in addressing worldly challenges through collective, action-oriented interfaith efforts to improve human conditions.

Sallie King, American scholar of religion, appropriately labels this "practical dialogue, in which the objective is to carry out a concrete project in the community or in the world . . . side-by-side with members of another religious community . . . to promote community harmony through people from different communities getting to know one another in a nonthreatening way."[33] King deems it "nonthreatening" probably because this method of engagement does not ask participants to surface their theological, spiritual, or worldview differences but rather invites them to collaborate on a shared project by drawing on the values and resources from their

33 Sallie B. King, "Interreligious Dialogue," in *The Oxford Handbook of Religious Diversity*, ed. Chad Meister (Oxford: Oxford University Press, 2011), 2.

own traditions. Russian thinker Sergey Melnik classifies praxis-oriented dialogue as "partnership dialogue" in which "followers of different religions carry out various joint activities" often with goals focusing on human need and rights, societal cohesion and flourishing, and environmental protection and ecological conservation.[34]

In 2017, the Dutch brewing company Heineken launched a television commercial called "Worlds Apart," which depicted several pairs of adults engaging in a "social experiment" from opposite ends of the spectrum on various divisive social issues such as climate change, transgender rights, and feminism. Each pair is given a flat-pack for a mysterious ready-to-assemble piece of furniture, which ends up being a countertop bar for serving beverages. Once assembled, each pair is confronted with the choice to "stay and discuss your differences over a beer" or to leave. In entertaining fashion, they all choose to stay, engage, listen, question, and encounter

34 Melnik, "Types of Interreligious Dialogue," 68–70.

each other over their differences. Though several lessons may be drawn from this fictitious and semi-humorous television sketch, a particularly powerful moment depicts the final words of the climate change denier enthusiastically agreeing with his counterpart, the environmental activist, that the productive thing to do is "To engage! To Engage!" (which is among the top lessons for dialogue in the next chapter). The joint activity of assembling a bar, which required putting aside ideological differences, to communicate and work collaboratively, helped them build trust to stay and discuss their differences.

Two people sitting together in silence, or working alongside one another in silence, can serve as a very powerful instance of dialogue. Hence, praxis-oriented dialogue may include various stakeholders and constituencies in a local neighborhood coming together in collaborative fashion to provide for those in need. While working alongside one another collaboratively, communities might not only work together but also engage in what is typically recognized as dialogue: verbal discussions. If such dialogue occurs, it often aligns with one or both of the next two distinct types: cognitive and existential.

Cognitive Dialogue

Cognitive dialogue emphasizes rational, intellectual engagement aimed at deepening understanding and uncovering truths through critical questioning and discourse. It serves as a methodical approach to explore and scrutinize ideas, philosophies, or religious doctrines to foster enlightenment and mutual insight among participants.

Leonard Swidler's "Dialogue of the Head"[35] or Sallie King's "verbal dialogue"[36] is perhaps what comes to mind for most people when they think of dialogue. This type seeks *the truth* and "a better understanding of another religion through a focus on a religion's doctrines, philosophy,

---

35 Swidler, *Dialogue for Interreligious Understanding*, 17.

36 King, "Interreligious Dialogue," 2.

theology, or worldview."[37] Within the Roman Catholic tradition, this type of dialogue was initially labeled "dialogue of specialists"[38] by Pope John Paul II and later became known as "dialogue of theological exchange, where specialists seek to deepen their understanding of their respective religious heritages, and to appreciate each other's spiritual values."[39] Although these official Catholic documents stress this dialogue as appropriate for specialists, it can and is appropriately undertaken by anyone regardless of expertise, training, or authority. Thus, it would seem, the broader labels of Melnik's "cognitive,"[40] King's "verbal," and Eric Sharpe's "discursive" are more suitable. Sharpe explains, "For those who assume that the human reason is competent to lead individuals into an understanding of truth, the activity previously called 'dialectic' or 'debate', when transmuted into

37 King, "Interreligious Dialogue," 2.

38 John Paul II, *The Attitude of the Church*, 31.

39 Pontifical Council for Inter-religious Dialogue, *Dialogue and Proclamation*, 42.

40 Melnik, "Types of Interreligious Dialogue," 58.

dialogical terms, may be characterized as 'discursive dialogue.' It involves meeting, listening and discussion on the level of mutual competent intellectual inquiry."[41]

Cognitive dialogue is sometimes referred to as Socratic since it entails "a dialectic of open, mutual questioning about something. Such dialogue is known to expose fresh understandings of the topic at hand."[42] Although many find verbal cognitive dialogue, or the dialogue of the intellect, engaging and interesting (though it's not for everyone), it is often the first thing that comes to mind when interfaith or interreligious dialogue is mentioned. However, it may not always be the most sustainable or significant,

---

41 Sharpe, "The Goals of Inter-Religious Dialogue," 82.

42 Richard W. Taylor, "The Meaning of Dialogue," in *Inter-religious Dialogue*, ed. Herbert Jai Singh (Bangalore: The Christian Institute for the Study of Religion and Society, 1967), 55; cited in Arvind Sharma, "The Meaning and Goals of Interreligious Dialogue," *Journal of Dharma* 8, no. 3 (1983): 228.

nor does it necessarily promise the greatest long-term impact and value, as discussed below.

Existential Dialogue

Existential dialogue explores the profound territories of personal and shared experiences of deep and ultimate meaning by going beyond cognitive discourse to explore the human existence through engagement with diverse spiritual practices and reflections on life's ultimate questions. Swidler's "Dialogue of the Heart"[43] and King's "spiritual" and "intervisitation" dialogues[44] seek *the beautiful* by learning about and engaging "in the spiritual practices of another religion, such as the other religion's form of prayer, meditation, or worship, or participates in a ritual together with members of another religion."[45] Within the Roman Catholic tradition, this type of dialogue is known as the "dialogue of religious

---

43 Swidler, *Dialogue for Interreligious Understanding*, 17.

44 King, "Interreligious Dialogue," 2.

45 King, "Interreligious Dialogue," 2.

experience, where persons, rooted in their own religious traditions, share their spiritual riches."[46] Sharpe identifies this type as *interior* dialogue and maintains the basic, sometimes implicit, assumption "that all intellectualization, doctrinal or otherwise, is of limited relevance, useful only as a means of approach to the divine mystery."[47] These forms of dialogue are *existential*, keeping in mind a literal working definition of *existential* to refer to that which is profoundly related to the ultimate depths and meaning of existence. Existential dialogue refers to learning and sharing experiences imbued with ultimate meaning and calls on individuals and communities to confront the purpose for their existence. Individuals need not be religiously affiliated or carry a defined religious identity to engage in this kind of dialogue. It is open to all, regardless of beliefs and practices or lack thereof. Many

46 John Paul II, *The Attitude of the Church*, 35; Pontifical Council for Inter-religious Dialogue, *Dialogue and Proclamation*, 42.

47 Sharpe, "The Goals of Inter-Religious Dialogue," 87.

(perhaps all) humans experience moments of ultimate meaning and significance, which some might refer to as *spiritual* or *sacred*. These may include traditional religious practices of prayer, mindfulness, and ritual; however, it may also include experiences of fishing, gardening, cooking, suffering, conversing with a close friend, surfing, being moved by music, experiencing art, undergoing the death of a friend or family member, or experiencing deep joy.

R. Scott Webster proposes an "existential framework of spirituality" as a model "that is not tied to religiosity."[48] In short, existential spirituality and dialogue are "able to transcend the religious/secular divide which so often is understood to be problematic when trying to promote spiritual development in non-religious contexts. This existential perspective can embrace both religious and non-religious views, and therefore

---

48 R. Scott Webster, "An Existential Framework of Spirituality," *International Journal of Children's Spirituality* 9, no. 1 (2004): 13.

it can be made available for all learners."[49] By characterizing this mode of dialogue as existential, access is broadened, allowing all people to articulate their experiences of profound and ultimate existential meaning, regardless of their religious affiliations and identities or lack thereof.

Humanizing Dialogue

Humanizing dialogue centers on fostering empathy, understanding, and respect through sharing the everyday experiences that define common humanity. It strives to put a unique human face on dialogue amid the vast messiness and complexity of life. Leonard Swidler's "Dialogue of Holiness,"[50] which seeks *the one*, is commonly referred to as "the *dialogue of life*" by the Roman Catholic Church (and others) and refers to "where people strive to live in an open and neighbourly spirit, sharing their

49 Webster, "An Existential Framework of Spirituality," 17.

50 Swidler, *Dialogue for Interreligious Understanding*, 17–18.

joys and sorrows, their human problems and preoccupations."[51] Above all, this type of dialogue strives to see the deep humanity in the other by putting a human face on the encounter and appealing to the common humanity of all persons. It is one of the most central, perhaps most important, forms of dialogue and thus echoes one of the most valuable lessons for dialogue offered in the next chapter: to always strive to humanize, humanize, humanize.

A recent team of scholars interviewed several interfaith dialogue participants, and one Pakistani participant made the astute observation that "a conservative with human quality works well. An intolerant progressive without human quality works badly. In the end, what is decisive, it's not the doctrinal orientation but the human disposition, the way of being, the capacity, the sensibility, the bonhomie . . . Can we have a homophobic in the group? Yes, if he has certain

---

51 John Paul II, *The Attitude of the Church*, 35; Pontifical Council for Inter-religious Dialogue, *Dialogue and Proclamation*, 42, *emphasis* original.

human qualities . . ., this human quality will change his perspective on homosexuality . . . as it has happened."[52]

Eric Sharpe refers to this form as "human" or "Buberian dialogue," referencing Martin Buber's dynamic and influential vision of dialogue. The central thrust of this type of dialogue is to put a unique human face on the other, acknowledging the imperfect and fragile state of being human in a world that we all know and experience in different, yet similar, ways. Thus, it sets doctrine, theology, belief, worldview, and practice aside to engage in human empathic connection. However, this is not to suggest that these things (doctrine, theology, belief, practice, etc.) are unimportant nor irrelevant. They can be relevant, and if they are not dealt with at some point, if necessary, they can fester and lead to greater confusion, misunderstanding, and stereotypes.

---

52 Roger Campdepadrós-Cullell, Miguel Ángel Pulido-Rodríguez, Jesús Marauri, and Sandra Racionero-Plaza, "Interreligious Dialogue Groups Enabling Human Agency," *Religions* 12, no. 3 (2021): 189.

Without a foundation in deeper human trust and communication rooted in seeing the common humanity in the other, such ideological exchange of the head can be more likely to falter, dissolve, or break down. When stronger relations are established on deeper trust (whether the parties involved are siblings, friends, acquaintances, or colleagues), disagreement, misunderstandings, ignorance, and ill-formed questions and comments can be absorbed, corrected, and transformed into empathetic learning experiences with greater charity and reconciliation.

Daryl Davis is a Black American professional musician and racial reconciliation expert and practitioner known for befriending white supremacist Ku Klux Klan members and convincing them to leave their racist ideology and ties behind. Davis almost naturally articulates and embodies these humanization aspects of dialogue. He says,

> Everybody I've met, no matter how different, is a human being. Everybody that I've

> encountered wants basically the same four things: they want to be loved, they want to be respected, they want to be heard, and they want the same thing for their family as we would want for our family. . . . Why do you hate me when you don't even know me? . . . We don't have to respect what people say, but we should respect their right to say it. Because if you don't respect their right to air their opinion, why should they listen to yours? . . . Don't ever disallow or disregard an opportunity for dialogue. A missed opportunity for dialogue is a missed opportunity for conflict resolution. And when two enemies are talking, they're not fighting. They're talking. It's when the conversation ceases, that the ground becomes fertile for violence. So, you want to keep the conversation going.[53]

---

53 Daryl Davis in *When in Doubt*, dir. by Travis Brown (Portland, OR, forthcoming), trailer videos published online, October 2020, https://www.facebook.com/whenindoubtfilm/videos.

The concept is simple and intuitive: greater trust to engage in deep conversation resides in relationships built on mutual respect, trust, listening, and seeing the human in the other. It is backed by recent social-scientific studies around the efficacy of bridge-building on the foundation of mutual trust, relationship, and ultimately friendship.

Humanizing dialogue—or the dialogue of life—need not focus initially on deep and potentially divisive ideological fissures such as politics, race, or religion. Rather, it rests on establishing deep human connections across those aspects of life to which we can all relate: sharing food, experiencing the joys and struggles of parenthood, coping with the loss of a loved one, celebrating the birth of a child, appreciating art, or starting a new job. As Davis preaches above, everybody is a human being with the desire for the same basic things and can relate to one another at deep foundational and human levels.

Ambassadorial Dialogue

Ambassadorial dialogue, though not as prominent as the other types, refers to various modes of dialogue, often commencing from communities coming together for dialogue or official religious leaders representing the communities. Marianne Moyaert, scholar of religion and comparative theology, refers to this type as *diplomatic interreligious dialogue*.[54] Other variations on this mode may include what King refers to as *official* or *institutional dialogue*, which takes place "between or among elites chosen by their religions as official representatives" or "*parliamentary-style dialogue* in which religious leaders speak in an open forum with the main objective of making their views widely known."[55] These modes of dialogue, although perhaps less common on local levels, remain important and influential. Moyaert astutely observes, "The importance of this form of dialogue has been questioned frequently. Doubt is raised about its

54 Moyaert, "Interreligious Dialogue," 202.

55 King, "Interreligious Dialogue," 2.

authenticity: can one speak here really about encounter as such? . . . [In this mode of dialogue,] one speaks, in the end, as a representative of one's tradition."[56] Although "these encounters are formal in nature" and unlikely to result in major religious institutional changes, they hold symbolic importance by showcasing "the willingness of religious leaders and their institutions to leave centuries-old hostility behind . . . meet one another, shake hands, receive one another hospitably, and sometimes even pray together [to] give a powerful signal to their respective adherents: strong faith convictions should not lead to interreligious animosity."[57] Thus, despite potential criticisms regarding its authenticity, ambassadorial dialogue can serve as a vital platform for religious leaders to demonstrate mutual respect and cooperation, setting a precedent for followers and contributing to a broader culture of interreligious understanding and learning.

56 Moyaert, "Interreligious Dialogue," 204.
57 Moyaert, "Interreligious Dialogue," 204.

Intrapersonal Dialogue

While most types of dialogue indicate an interpersonal mode of encounter between two or more people, *intrapersonal dialogue* occurs during and beyond such encounters. Intrapersonal dialogue refers to the interior self-reflective dialogue that takes place within an individual. King refers to it as that "internal dialogue, in which a single individual has an internal conversation going on between two religions to which he or she has been exposed, ordinarily at some depth and over some time."[58] Raimon Panikkar famously calls this *the intrareligious dialogue*, or that dialogue that takes "place in the depths of the person"[59] and in which one struggles with oneself and helps "us to discover the 'other' in ourself."[60] Intrapersonal dialogue, as described by King and Panikkar, underscores the profound personal journey of reconciling

58 King, "Interreligious Dialogue," 2.

59 Raimon Panikkar, *The Intrareligious Dialogue*, rev. ed. (New York: Paulist Press, 1999), xvii.

60 Panikkar, *The Intrareligious Dialogue*, xix.

and integrating diverse religious influences within oneself, demonstrating the significance of internal exploration in understanding and embracing the diversity of one's own (non)religious identity.

DIALOGUE BEYOND DEBATE

Much is made of what dialogue is, but much is also made of what dialogue is not. Scholars and practitioners often preach that dialogue is not just conversation, discussion, training or education, propaganda, negotiations, deliberation, conferencing, advocacy, or consultation. Although there is no consensus about any precise clear and distinct boundaries among all of these in relation to dialogue, it is accurate to assert that almost all seem to agree that dialogue is most certainly not debate. While most agree that dialogue is not the same as debate, others make more subtle distinctions between dialogue and the following concepts:

DIALOGUE VS. OTHER CONCEPTS

- ***Propaganda:*** For Bryn, Edisvåg, and Skurdal of the Nansen Center for Peace and Dialogue, "Where propaganda seeks to persuade the other, we seek to understand each other through dialogue. Whilst we try to win over others through debate, we seek to overcome our own stereotypes and enemy images though dialogue."[1]
- ***Advocacy:*** For the KAICIID Dialogue Centre, "Dialogue is not 'advocacy': in advocacy, the objective is to rally support for your idea or a certain idea or action in general. Therefore, the intention is to convince others that our own idea and perception is the best. In dialogue, there is no intention or pressure to convince anyone about anything, in any direction. It is all about increased mutual understanding for better learning about

1 Bryn et al., "What Is Dialogue?" 11.

each other firstly, and possibly about a given topic secondarily, if the dialogue includes a specific one."[2]

- ***Consultation***: For the KAICIID Dialogue Centre, "Dialogue is not 'consultation': in a consultation, the organizers get the participants to share their feedback or opinions on certain topics, sometimes to identify their needs or to come up with solutions. Dialogue is not a relationship between a beneficiary and a service provider where feedback is needed in one direction only."[3]
- ***Conferencing***: For the KAICIID Dialogue Centre, "Dialogue is not a 'conference': in a conference, people come to share their theories and statements in a formal setting. Dialogue is less formal and definitely not a forum for sharing theories and make general statements. In dialogue, participants are encouraged

2 Abu-Nimer et al., *Building Bridges*, 23.
3 Abu-Nimer et al., *Building Bridges* 23.

to share the personal understanding and questions about each other. At the same time, a conference may include elements of dialogue and nowadays, many conferences benefit from using dialogue methodology in some, if not all, sessions."[4]

- ***Negotiation***: For the KAICIID Dialogue Centre, "Dialogue is not a 'negotiation': in a negotiation, the parties come with the aim (and pressure) of reaching an agreement. In dialogue, the intention is to learn about another person or party's perceptions and understandings of a topic without the pressure of reaching a solution."[5] For Bryn, Edisvåg, and Skurdal, "Whilst we attempt to reach agreement through negotiations, we try to understand through dialogue. A better understanding of the other also entails a deeper understanding of

4 Abu-Nimer et al., *Building Bridges* 22.
5 Abu-Nimer et al., *Building Bridges* 23.

myself. I become aware that I could have been the other."[6]

- ***Deliberation***: Daniel Yankelovich, a well-known American social researcher and public opinion analyst, considers deliberation "a form of thought and reflection that can take place in any kind of conversation."[7] "It is a problem solving activity involving the weighing up of different options. This activity can happen, according to Yankelovich, in dialogue as well as in discussion or debate. It is only when imminent consensus and decision become the priority of the conversation that dialogue's essential focus on mutual understanding gets lost. Dialogue, though it often leads to decision-making processes, must be kept

---

6 Bryn et al., "What Is Dialogue?" 11.

7 Daniel Yankelovich, *The Magic of Dialogue* (New York: Simon and Schuster, 1999), 45; cited in Sleap and Sener, *Dialogue Theories*, 175.

separate from these for each to function properly."[8]

- ***Training or Education:*** For Lisa Schirch and David Campt, "Training helps people learn something, usually by transferring knowledge from the trainer to the student. Learning also happens in dialogue, but not through a direct transfer. Dialogue helps people generate their own new collective understanding of a situation through exchanges between participants."[9]
- ***Discussion***: For David Bohm, "The main difference between dialogue and discussion is that in much ordinary discussion the participants have fixed positions and they present their own views and try to convince others to change their perspective. This approach often

---

8 Sleap and Sener, *Dialogue Theories*, 175–76.

9 Schirch and Campt, *The Little Book of Dialogue*, 7.

creates tension, confrontation and distrust among the participants. These features are all harmful to the dialogic process, hindering 'free play of thought' among discussants. The dynamics of such a discussion obstruct the participants' ability to think creatively."[10] For Schirch and Campt, "In a discussion, information and ideas are exchanged in order to accomplish a specific task or to solve a problem. The intention of dialogue is not to accomplish a task, even though a dialogue process sometimes identifies follow-up tasks."[11] For Yankelovich, "The relationship between dialogue and discussion is more subtle. Talk becomes dialogue rather than just discussion when three particular conditions are in place. Firstly, there must be

---

10 Sleap and Sener, *Dialogue Theories*, 39.

11 Schirch and Campt, *The Little Book of Dialogue*, 7.

equality between the participants and an absence of coercive influences. . . . Secondly, dialogue requires us to listen with empathy. . . . Finally, in dialogue participants need to explore their own assumptions and those of others, and bring them out into the open. . . . Discussion does not necessarily require equality, listening with empathy or the exploration of assumptions, but these three conditions the marks of dialogue."[12]

- ***Conversation:*** For Schirch and Campt, "In conversation, information and ideas flow between people for the primary purpose of self-expression. Persuasion, or changing another's perspective or understanding, may not figure into the exchange. Unlike conversation, a specific goal of dialogue is to broaden participant's understanding of a particular

12 Sleap and Sener, *Dialogue Theories*, 174–75.

issue."[13] For Buber, "Dialogue is not a kind of conversation but a mode of being in relation to others. When two people meet in the I-You encounter of dialogue they perceive each other as whole persons, not as things to be understood, negotiated with or used. Dialogue as described by Buber has immense importance in human life."[14] For the KAICIID Dialogue Centre, "Dialogue is not a 'conversation': in a conversation, the persons engaged are simply talking with each other in a longer exchange of words, often focused on a particular topic, but open to change. There is not objective of any kind."[15]

---

13 Schirch and Campt, *The Little Book of Dialogue*, 7.

14 Sleap and Sener, *Dialogue Theories*, 58.

15 Abu-Nimer et al., *Building Bridges* 22.

As shown in table 2.1 below, which draws from experienced dialogue scholars and practitioners from around the world,[61] there are several rigorously systematic accounts that distinguish dialogue from debate. In general, while dialogue seeks understanding, listening, learning, collaborating, and finding common ground, debate seeks winning, convincing, competing, and arguing. While dialogue promotes openness to change, self-critique, and the re-evaluation of one's own ideas, debate seeks to defend one's prior assumptions and find errors in the view of the other. While dialogue is often characterized by tolerance and acceptance, debate often centers on moral judgment and condemnation of opposing views. While in dialogue, emotions are often welcome as appropriate means through which to convey personal experience and viewpoints, debate sometimes portrays emotions as a sign of

---

61 Schirch and Campt, *The Little Book of Dialogue for Difficult Subjects*; Abu-Nimer et al., *Building Bridges*; Paula Green, *Peacebuilding in Divided Communities* (Amherst, MA: Karuna Center for Peacebuilding, 2012); and Bryn et al., "What Is Dialogue?".

poor rationale, or if emotions are deployed, they might be used as means to intimidate the opposition. While dialogue seeks to build bridges across gulfs of difference, debate seeks to determine who is on the right side of the gulf in the first place.

Daryl Davis teaches,

> Learn as much as you can about the other person's ideology, their position, on whatever it is you are going to converse about. Do not frame it as a debate, because as soon as you say the word "debate" people get their dander up and they're ready to fight and argue and whatever else. Frame it as a conversation. . . . Put yourself in their shoes. Try to see it from their perspective. The more you know about them and how they think, the better off you'll be to give them persuading thoughts that will make them reevaluate. . . . Even though they may not like you, they will respect you as soon as they see you've done your homework and you know a lot about this.[62]

62 Davis in *When in Doubt.*

TABLE 2.1 DIALOGUE AND DEBATE

DIALOGUE	
Schirch & Campt	**KAICIID**
The goal is to understand different perspectives and learn about other views	Collaborative approach
People listen to others to understand how their experiences shape their beliefs	The parties are working together toward a common understanding.
People accept the experiences of others as real and valid	One assumes there is possibly more than one "right answer" and that each person may therefore only have "part of the answer" or a perspective on it
People appear to be somewhat open to expanding their understanding of the issue	Finding common ground is the goal
People speak primarily from their own understanding and experience	One communicates at the levels of interests, needs, feelings, and values
People work together toward common understanding	One listens to the other side in order to understand
Strong emotions like anger and sadness are appropriate when they convey the intensity of an experience or a belief	Reveals assumptions for re-evaluation
	Causes introspection of one's own position
	Opens the possibility of reaching a better solution than any of the originally imagined solutions
	Creates an open-minded attitude, an openness to being wrong and to change
	Prompts a search for basic agreements
	Involves a real concern for the other person and does not seek to alienate or offend

Karuna Center	Nansen Center
Goal is to discover common ground	The goal is to understand
Involves listening to understand points	Explain/tell
Involves openly considering all points of view	Listen before talking
Assumes that many different ideas can contribute to a fuller solution	Look for the counterpart's strength
Expresses feelings, concerns, fears, and uncertainties	Make the counterpart feel safe
Demonstrates strengths on all sides of an issue	Tolerance /self-discipline/ self-criticism
Uncovers brand-new possibilities and opportunities	
Builds bridges of understanding	
Promotes collaboration over competition	

TABLE 2.1 DIALOGUE AND DEBATE (*continued*)

DEBATE	
Schirch & Campt	**KAICIID**
Goal is to "win" the argument by affirming one's own views and discrediting other views	Oppositional approach
People listen to others to find flaws in their arguments	Each party is trying to prove their own point or prove the other wrong
People critique the experiences of others as distorted and invalid	One assumes there is one right answer
People appear to be determined not to change their own views on the issue	Winning is the goal; a win-lose approach
People speak based on assumptions made about others' positions and motivations	One communicates through a predetermined position
People oppose each other and attempt to prove each other wrong.	One listens to the other side in order to find flaws and to counter its arguments
Strong emotions like anger are often used to intimidate the other side	Defends assumptions as the truth
	Causes critique of the other position
	Defends one's own positions as the best solutions and excludes other solutions
	Creates a closed-minded attitude, a determination to be right
	Prompts a search for glaring differences
	Involves a countering of the other position without focusing on feelings or relationships and often belittles or deprecates the other person

Karuna Center	Nansen Center
Goal is to win	Goal is to win
Involves listening to find the opponent's weak points	Convince/argue
Involves criticizing other points of view	Talk before listening
Assumes one right answer to a question or problem	Searching for the other's weak argument
Comes from a position that one defends	Making the counterpart insecure
Exposes faults in the positions of others	Moral judgment
Looks to strengthen a predetermined position	Confrontational body language
Further polarizes antagonistic positions	To change one's opinion is a sign of weakness
Promotes competition over collaboration	

These are broad strokes about dialogue and debate, and the goal here is not to demonize debate and glorify dialogue. Debate remains important and can serve constructive purposes. Debate may even have a place within various dialogues, depending on the context, circumstances, and trust among the participants. While most agree that dialogue is not the same as debate, others make subtler distinctions between dialogue and the activities listed on pages 62–69.

Having introduced the necessity ("the why") and nature ("the what") of dialogue, the subsequent chapters delve into the crucial aspects of practicing effective communication ("the how") and explore traditional insights that have withstood the test of time (i.e., proverbial wisdom).

CHAPTER THREE

Practical Communication

As the peacock devours poisonous plants only to transform their toxins into the colorful spectrum evident in its feathers, dialogue can serve as a tool to learn, understand, and transform potentially toxic situations of misunderstanding and conflict into life-giving and peaceful connections. While the previous chapter introduced the nature of dialogue and mapped its multiple modes, this chapter offers concrete guidelines for transformative dialogue. These include humanize always, engage, avoid essentialism, embrace humility, and employ promising practices. This chapter aims to equip readers with the skills and insights necessary for engaging in a meaningful dialogue in order to transform challenges into opportunities for growth and understanding.

A NECESSARY PRELIMINARY: "RULES ARE FOR FOOLS"

Sage advice is offered at the beginning of the exercise manual for dialogue facilitators and trainers prepared by Paula Green and the Karuna Center for Peacebuilding, an American organization that empowers communities divided by conflict to achieve mutual understanding and sustainable peace through dialogue, training, and collaborative peacebuilding initiatives: "Too frequently trainers, especially those with fewer years of experience, use exercises as an anchor of their program, rather than aids to their teaching. Peacebuilding programs and selected tools should be rooted in the goals of the training and based on the stated needs of the communities in which the training will be offered. Please use these tools with discernment for local particularities and group needs."[1]

Using overly rigid templates as crutches or anchors is a rather common habit among novices in many settings, not just dialogue facilitation and conflict mediation. The same may be equally said of teachers and instructors who rely too heavily on predetermined curricula to the extent that they forgo opportunities to adapt learning experiences to the chemistry, context, and interests of their students. Hence, a necessary preliminary to any set of dialogue guidelines cautions that "rules are for fools."[2]

This is not to suggest that guidelines are counterproductive and should be discarded

---

1 Paula Green, *Peacebuilding in Divided Communities* (Amherst, MA: Karuna Center for Peacebuilding, 2012), 14.

2 See Hans Gustafson, "Letting Go," in *Teaching Interreligious Encounter*, ed. Marc A. Pugliese and Alexander Y. Hwang (New York: Oxford University Press, 2017), 141–42.

at all costs. Rather, it is to suggest remaining conscious of the practice that rules can be shed, broken, or discarded if they hinder the group or goal. Moreover, it is to suggest that ultimately not only should ground rules for dialogue be generated by the participants themselves but these rules ought to be revisited, revised, and reconsidered as dialogue wears on. Hence, the call here that "rules are for fools" is a rallying cry for dialogue participants and facilitators to remain ever vigilant to build into their program a natural flexibility and agility for the dialogue process.

HUMANIZE, HUMANIZE, HUMANIZE

The "humanize, humanize, humanize" principle stands as the most important teaching of dialogue and encounter. It asserts that the paramount principle in any interaction is to always recognize and respect others as individual humans with inherent dignity. This fundamental ethos not only transcends but also informs all other aspects of communication, conflict resolution, and transformation. To humanize others is to holistically see them in all their unique and complicated ways beyond any superficial attributes (hair color) and group identities (ethnicity, race, gender, etc.), although these group identities need not be ignored when considering how they have contributed and continue to contribute to oppressive and unjust structures and responses that frame one's own self-identity or self-worth. Jenn Lindsay, American social scientist, documentary filmmaker, and musician, observes, "Humanization is a frequently invoked concept in the interreligious world"[3] with dialogue practitioners often invoking "'humanity' as an aspirational ideal, [with] humanity . . . contrasted with the natural tendency to conflict and social bias that dialoguers say is found

3 Jenn Lindsay, "Interfaith Dialogue and Humanization of the Religious Other," *International Journal of Interreligious and Intercultural Studies* 3, no. 2 (2020): 1.

among human beings."[4] Thus, Lindsay's insights highlight the critical importance of this teaching in encounters across difference, underscoring the necessity of seeing each individual beyond group identities and biases and recognizing their unique humanity as the foundation for effective communication and meaningful understanding.

This teaching approaches dialogue by focusing not on official organizational, formal, or institutional memberships and identities (such as religious, cultural, geographical, linguistic, or national) but rather by starting with the unique individuality of the human person in the everyday "here and now" of each encounter. Lindsey recognizes that "one might say that the direct opposite of humanization is dehumanization. Dehumanization can run the gamut from active oppression and violence, or, in its lighter form, to stereotyping and silencing."[5] Stereotyping is among the subtler, yet frequent, forms of

---

4 Lindsay, "Interfaith Dialogue," 6.
5 Lindsay, "Interfaith Dialogue," 5.

dehumanization as it identifies an individual with group identities and often in inaccurate and offensive ways. Focusing on the humanity of the individual extends an opportunity for dismantling and discarding oppressive and distorted group identities. As one Catholic nun observed, "At the heart of our dialogue is respect for the dignity of the individual."[6] Likewise, another dialogue practitioner notes, "We're all humans. We suffer, we love, get angry, get sad. We can believe in different things, but we all have the same feelings. If we can see this, we can love each other. Ideas are different so we can't connect there. But we can connect on a human level."[7]

This echoes the guiding sentiment from Steinar Bryn and others at the Nansen Center for Peace and Dialogue to not "begin the dialogue with the viewpoints and arguments. Begin with the faces, the shared meals, the life histories. . . . share experiences about what it

6 Cited in Lindsay, "Interfaith Dialogue," 9.
7 Cited in Lindsay, "Interfaith Dialogue," 10.

means to be a human being."[8] Hence, the humanize, humanize, humanize teaching's emphasis on individual human experience as the starting point for dialogue reflects a universal truth: recognizing and respecting our shared humanity is the key to transcending stereotypes and biases, fostering understanding and building respect.

Humans are incredibly complex. When people oversimplify others and reduce them to superficial or group identities, they can stereotype and essentialize them. They dehumanize them or, worse yet, demonize them. Daryl Davis, dialogue practitioner and racial reconciliation practitioner, asks, "Where has demonizing anyone gotten us? All we have to do is turn on our TV and look out in our streets. . . . We need to come together because we have a shared history. And it's important that we know each other's history. And when you get to know somebody,

---

8 Steinar Bryn, Inge Edisvåg, and Ingunn Skurdall, "What Is Dialogue?" in *Understanding the Other: Dialogue as a Tool and an Attitude to Life* (Lillehammer: Nansen Fredssenter, 2015), 16.

it's very hard to hate them. So it's time that we get to know one another."[9] Davis's comment pertains to the particular divides in the United States; however, his point transcends this context: knowing someone—establishing a personal relationship with them—is a step toward humanization and respect.

Rabbi Rachel S. Mikva, a thought leader in the field of interreligious studies and engagement, draws attention to Diana Eck's recounting of a story. Eck, professor of Indian religions and founder and director of the Pluralism Project at Harvard University, details an incident about a prayer guide published by the International Mission Board of the Southern Baptist Convention in the United States. The guide directed Baptists to pray during the Hindu fall festival of Diwali because, according to the publication, Hindus are "lost in the hopeless darkness of Hinduism . . . who

---

9 Daryl Davis in *When in Doubt*, dir. by Travis Brown (Portland, OR, forthcoming), trailer videos published online, October 2020, https://www.facebook.com/whenindoubtfilm/videos.

worship gods which are not God."[10] As Mikva points out in her book *Dangerous Religious Ideas*, Eck leans into a humanizing approach in her model to confront this potentially dangerous religious idea voiced by her fellow Christians. Eck's envisioned response is worth repeating here in its entirety:

> To the Southern Baptists who published their prayer guide for Hindus whom they deemed lost in hopeless darkness, I might say something like this. "As a scholar of Hinduism, I must say you have seriously misrepresented the Hindu tradition in the ways in which you portray it in your publication and I would be happy to speak with you about where I think your portrayal is misleading. As an American

---

10 *Divali: Festival of Lights Prayer for Hindus* (Richmond, VA: International Mission Board of the Southern Baptist Convention, 1990); cited in Diana L. Eck, "Prospects for Pluralism," *Journal of the American Academy of Religion* 75, no. 4 (2007): 752, https://doi.org/10.1093/jaarel/lfm061; cited in Rachel S. Mikva, *Dangerous Religious Ideas* (Boston: Beacon Press, 2020), 197–8.

> and fellow citizen, however, I will defend your right to believe and practice Christianity as you do, to believe the worst about our Hindu neighbors, to believe they are all going to hell, and to say so, both privately and publicly. But as a Christian, let me challenge you here, for I believe that your views of our neighbors are not well grounded in the Gospel of Christ, as I understand it."[11]

As Mikva recognizes, Eck's response does not demonize, dehumanize, or disparage the Southern Baptists, but rather it challenges them to rethink their position. Without *contemning* (disrespecting) the person, she *condemns* (disapproves of) their ideas, leaving intact respect and freedom for those she challenges.[12] Davis phrases the spirit of Eck's response as follows:

---

11 Eck, "Prospects for Pluralism," 771.

12 Mikva, *Dangerous Religious Ideas*, 197–98. For drawing attention to the critical distinction between *condemn* and *contemn*, Mikva credits Cathleen Kaveny, *Prophecy without Contempt* (Cambridge, MA: Harvard University Press, 2016), ix–x.

"We don't have to respect what people say, but we should respect their right to say it. Because if you don't respect their right to air their opinion, why should they listen to yours?"[13] The titanium teaching to humanize complements the next guideline for practical communication across difference, which is the diamond directive of dialogue to engage!

ENGAGE!

The 2017 Heineken television commercial "Worlds Apart," mentioned in the previous chapter, depicts several pairs of adults from the United Kingdom engaging in a "social experiment" from opposite ends of the spectrum on various divisive social issues, such as climate change, transgender rights, and feminism. Each pair is given a flatpack for a mysterious ready-to-assemble piece of furniture, which

---

13 Davis in *When in Doubt.*

ends up being a countertop bar for serving beverages. Once assembled, each pair is confronted with the choice to "stay and discuss your differences over a beer" or to leave. They all choose to stay, engage, listen, question, and encounter each other over their differences. The final words of the climate-change denier convey the enthusiastic agreement with his counterpart, the environmental activist, that the productive thing to do is "To engage! To Engage!"

The Council for Religions and Life Stance Communities in Norway (STL), which is an umbrella organization that brings together religious and life stance communities, published a "dialogue poster" displaying nine best practices for interreligious dialogue. A three-page "explainer" accompanies the poster, with deeper explanations offered for these practices. The document ends with a short paragraph, the heading of which reads "The Golden Rule of dialogue:

Engagement!"[14] A "golden rule" can be articulated in several ways; however, the general spirit of it is to treat others as you prefer them to treat you, or in the more flexible version from Confucius, "Do not impose on others what you do not wish for yourself."[15] The suggestion from STL is to engage others in a manner they would want to be engaged in and in ways we feel comfortable engaging.

Regardless of the approach one takes in treating others, engagement is essential. Dialogues will not succeed simply by gathering people together and adhering to prescribed methods. Plurality and diversity of viewpoints and

---

14 Helge Svare in cooperation with the Council for Religious and Life Stance Communities, "Explanation of the Dialogue Poster," Council for Religious and Life Stance Communities, Oslo, 2017, 4.

15 Consider the more nuanced "platinum rule" of "do unto others as they themselves would have done unto them." While the Golden Rule advises treating others as you would like to be treated, and Confucius's Silver Rule suggests not imposing on others what you would not desire for yourself, the Platinum Rule proposes treating others as they would prefer to be treated.

voices do not ensure genuine engagement without effort and openness from all participants. Rather, dialogue requires "participants to have a dialogue mindset."[16] Diana Eck asserts that pluralism is not diversity alone; rather, it is the energetic engagement with diversity. In fact, diversity alone can, and often does, lead to negative outcomes. As Eck and the Pluralism Project at Harvard University teach, "Diversity can and has meant the creation of religious ghettoes with little traffic between or among them. . . . Mere diversity without real encounter and relationship will yield increasing tensions in our societies."[17] Therefore, true pluralism and productive dialogue demand not only the presence of diverse voices but also a commitment to meaningful interaction, fostering an environment where differences are not just tolerated but actively explored and respected.

---

16 Svare, "Explanation of the Dialogue Poster," 4.

17 "What Is Pluralism?" The Pluralism Project, accessed April 1, 2021, https://pluralism.org/about.

Pope Francis, to a significant degree, has made his papacy about cultivating what he calls a "*culture of encounter*, capable of transcending our differences and divisions."[18] He calls his fellow Roman Catholics to "be passionate about meeting others, seeking points of contact, building bridges, planning a project that includes everyone."[19] This is not a beckoning forth of everyone to join hands and reach a consensus on all things. Rather, it is encouragement to examine obstacles that prevent bridge-building and, in their place, "create *processes* of encounter, processes that build a people that can accept differences."[20] Francis proclaims, "Let us arm our children with the weapons of dialogue! Let us teach them to fight the good fight of the culture of encounter!"[21]

---

18 Pope Francis, *Fratelli Tutti* (Vatican City: Libreria Editrice Vaticana, 2020), 215.

19 Pope Francis, *Fratelli Tutti*, 216.

20 Pope Francis, *Fratelli Tutti*, 217 *emphasis* original.

21 Pope Francis, *Fratelli Tutti*,.

This concept of dialogue to engage aligns with Patricia Ryan Madson's first maxim of life lessons from *Improv Wisdom*, explored in the next chapter: "Say Yes." This principle embodies courage and optimism, inviting collaboration and openness. It's about embracing the spirit of saying yes to opportunities for engagement, understanding, and bridge-building, expanding our world through the power of positive and inclusive interaction.[22]

ESSENTIALISM IS TOXIC

In the context of religion and interreligious encounters, *essentialism* refers to the idea of defining a religious tradition or personal identity's core ("essence") as unchanging and fixed. Following this logic, it also implies that any conditions deemed necessary and sufficient for one specific religious tradition or identity must

---

22 Patricia Ryan Madson, *Improv Wisdom* (New York: Bell Tower, 2005), 27.

be universally applicable to all members within that same tradition or identity. In simpler terms, essentializing the other is to oversimplify their identity by assuming that all those with the same tradition or identity must be identical in practice, worldview, and ideology. Of course, we all know from personal experience that this is not the case.

Although the problematic tendency to essentialize religious traditions and identities (especially traditions and identities other than one's own) has long been acknowledged in the academic study of religion, it remains a persistent reality and challenge among everyday interreligious encounter and sometimes, as Rachel Mikva observes, "despite the experience and sophistication" of scholars and practitioners, at formal and informal interfaith gatherings.[23] Martin Stringer, scholar of religion, researched what happened

---

23 See Rachel S. Mikva, "Six Issues That Complicate Interreligious Studies and Engagement," in *Interreligious/Interfaith Studies: Defining a New Field*, ed. Eboo Patel, Jennifer Howe Peace, and Noah Silverman (Boston: Beacon Press, 2018), 131–33.

when a local interfaith dialogue group, the Birmingham Conversations, in Birmingham, England, focused on lived religious everyday experiences.[24] One of Stringer's main observations was that by focusing on the lived everyday religious experiences (opposed to beliefs of a tradition), the dialogue group more easily overcame the temptation to essentialize each other. That is, they were more quickly able to recognize when they unfairly cast blanket stereotypes or misconceptions onto their co-participants. Stringer noted that at the outset of the study, many of the non-Muslim participants would treat Muslims as a monolithic single entity sharing all the same common (essential) features and thus labeling and judging them collectively instead of as individuals. The focus on lived experience helped quickly complicate matters (in a good way) by focusing on the individual uniqueness of each

24 Martin D. Stringer, "Lived Religion and Difficult Conversations," Birmingham Conversations of the Faith, Neighbors, Changemakers Collaboration, Birmingham, 2015, 4.

person and thus shattering any preconceived or assumed essentialist tendencies.

The notion that essentialism is toxic upholds a tip for good dialogue from Bryn and others at the Nansen Center, which states, "Do not ascribe viewpoints to others which they do not have,"[25] such as "all Muslims believe X, all Jews practice Y, or all Christians prohibit Z." For "no one should have to wriggle in the definition net of others ('After all, you Muslims think that . . .'). No one should have to defend viewpoints they don't themselves have."[26] Likewise, the Nansen Center's *Handbook for Trainers in Dialogue and Conflict Transformation* teaches about the very real dehumanizing dangers of placing and judging people in groups and categories: "Categorizing is often inaccurate and misleading, and will always be based on imperfect information and filtered by others' background and life experiences. The consequences can be extremely dangerous, as we have

25 Bryn et al., "What Is Dialogue?" 17.
26 Bryn et al., "What Is Dialogue?" 17.

seen in many conflicts where groups have been associated with identifying traits, which have result in exclusion or genocide (Jews in Germany, Muslims many places in Europe)."[27] This understanding helps participants recognize and practice the profound humility often necessary to avoid the dehumanizing dangers of essentializing people.

EMBRACE HUMILITY

As the popular proverb (often attributed to Confucius) goes, "If you're the smartest person in the room, then you're in the wrong room." Or perhaps "then you need to find a new room." Or maybe even "then consider embracing humility." With due respect to the wisdom attributed to Confucius's proverb, if you're the smartest person in the room, then you may not be in the

27 Norunn Grande and Christiane Seehausen, eds., *The Nansen Handbook for Trainers in Dialogue and Conflict Transformation* (Lillehammer: Nansen Fredssenter, 2018), 28.

wrong room after all, but rather you ought to consider adopting a humbler framework for learning and dialogue.

Embracing humility, put simply, teaches to always assume we have something to learn from everyone.[28] Humility has taken on several colloquial definitions such as showing modesty, exhibiting reluctance to accept honors or deserved recognition, putting others before yourself, being teachable, or lacking arrogance. Some of these definitions, though not wrong, are closer than others to the radical or root-derived definition of humility, which refers to having a realistic sense of one's own limits of knowing and talents.

The Nansen Center for Peace and Dialogue's *Handbook for Trainers in Dialogue and Conflict Transformation* identifies humility as one of three

28 Others have pointed out similar formulations: e.g., rule 9 of Jordan Peterson's *12 Rules for Life* (Toronto: Penguin Random House Canada, 2018); Diane Millis, ed., "Learn from Everyone," in *Deepening Engagement* (Woodstock, VT: Skylight Paths, 2015), 91–94.

basic principles[29] for dialogue, and Catherine Cornille deems humility one among five major essential conditions necessary for constructive and enriching dialogue, especially between and among people with various religious identities. Cornille teaches that in dialogue, "humble awareness of the finite and partial nature of one's own understanding [is what] drives one from the same to the other, from complacency to an active search for growth in the truth."[30] Humility is what Belgian comparative theologian and scholar of religion Marianne Moyaert defines as a "certain awareness of one's own limitations, a certain humility is . . . an important requirement for the success of interreligious dialogue that also entails the possibility of growth in faith."[31]

29 Grande and Seehausen, eds., *The Nansen Handbook*, 9.

30 Catherine Cornille, *The Im-Possibility of Interreligious Dialogue* (New York: Crossroad Publishing, 2008), 9.

31 Marianne Moyaert, "Interreligious Dialogue," in *Understanding Interreligious Relations*, ed. David Cheetham, Douglas Pratt, and David Thomas (Oxford: Oxford University Press, 2013), 212.

Being humble entails the attitude of actively seeking to challenge one's own assumptions and knowledge by being open and perhaps assuming something can always be learned from everyone.

Humility, especially intellectual humility—the recognition and acceptance of one's limitations and fallibility in knowledge—is not only a mark of constructive engagement and self-awareness but also a trait that marks a flourishing life. Eranda Jayawickreme, psychology professor and scholar of happiness, personality, character, and well-being, argues that intellectual humility is among the few traits that ensure one understands the world the way it really is. He explains, "Being intellectually humble involves understanding your cognitive limitations—in simpler terms, it means acknowledging that you could be wrong about something. If you're not open to acknowledging that you could be wrong, you can't learn anything new about the world; you're not going to be able to change your beliefs and grow."[32] Embracing intellectual humility is not just about self-improvement; rather, it is also a fundamental step toward a deeper, more accurate comprehension of the ever-changing world around.

PROMISING PRACTICES

Dialogue, while theoretically straightforward, can often be severely difficult and challenging in practice. This is particularly true for those not raised in traditions, families, cultures, or households that value and practice successful dialogue principles and approaches. Dialogue's complexity[33] should not be underestimated, and as such,

---

32 Eranda Jayawickreme, "The Power of Intellectual Humility," *Psychology Today*, April 13, 2022, https://www.psychologytoday.com/us/blog/pathways-flourishing/202204/the-power-intellectual-humility.

33 Karsten Lehmann, "Interreligious Dialogue in Context: Towards a Systematic Comparison of IRD-Activities in Europe," *Interdisciplinary Journal for Religion and Transformation in Contemporary Society* 6 (2020): 240.

it warrants a substantial treatment of guidelines for constructive engagement. In addition to the major principles sketched above, the following insights about dialogue also deserve recognition.

Articulate Goals and Aims

Having clearly articulated goals and aims helps ensure that all actors are generally on the same page while avoiding potential misunderstandings that may surface down the road. Furthermore, inviting all involved parties into the process of articulating goals from the outset helps create a more equal playing field. As discussed in the first chapter, there is no perfect consensus on the goals and aims of interreligious dialogue. Rather, these should be generated and agreed on by the group at the outset. Different participants of the same dialogue or encounter may come in with different goals and expectations, and this can sometimes work out just fine. Some may have personal goals of being seen, heard, and acknowledged, while others may have the goal of listening to and learning from the stories and experiences of others. This divergence in goals need not be problematic as long as, to the extent that it is possible, the goals are not veiled or function as ulterior motives (i.e., avoid hiding the agenda). Sometimes it may not be apparent what the goals are at the outset, and the process of engagement and dialogue will help initiate the process of articulating those goals. Likewise, goals may change as time goes on and as participants develop relationships and grow with one another. In short, there is no hard and fast blueprint or rigid set of what dialogue goals ought to be. Rather, the idea is that the goals are best generated, articulated, challenged, revised, and nuanced by all participants involved.

Embrace Co-creation

Embracing a co-creative elicitive (Socratic) model refers to adopting a model of dialogue and encounter that begins with the premise that all the wisdom and knowledge to set healthy and constructive parameters for the experience already reside within the group of participants involved. This constitutes Spanish-Catalan philosopher and theologian Raimon Panikkar's second principle for constructive intercultural and interreligious encounter: "The rules for the encounter are given and ground in the encounter itself. They cannot be fixed a priori by any of the single parties to the exclusion of the other."[34] What is more, it assumes the likelihood that all or most of the knowledge and resources for learning already rest with the active participants. The number-one tip from Bryn and colleagues is to "invite the participants to the planning"[35] and share ownership of the process by making it

34 Raimon Panikkar, "Some Notes on Syncretism and Eclecticism: Related to the Growth of Human Consciousness," in *Opera Omnia, Vol. 6: Cultures and Religions in Dialogue, Part One: Pluralism and Interculturality*, ed. Milena Carrara Pavan (Maryknoll, NY: Orbis Books, 2018), 96; first published in *Religious Syncretism in Antiquity: Essays in Conversation with Geo Widengren*, ed. B. A. Pearson (Missoula, MT: Scholars Press, 1975), 47–62.

35 Bryn et al., "What Is Dialogue?" 16.

a joint project with no hidden agendas, ulterior goals, or manipulative undermining. Inspired by Freire (from above) that dialogue is best guided by the experiences of the participants themselves and that those involved are the best experts, John Paul Lederach's "integrated framework" for conflict resolution training rests on several central ideas, among them that "people in a setting are a key resource, not recipients. . . . Building from available local resources fosters self-sufficiency and sustainability. Empowerment involves a process that fosters awareness-of-self in context and validates discovery, naming, and creation through reflection and action."[36] As noted in the previous chapter, Socrates modeled the elicitive model by utilizing the tool of dialogue to pull the already existing knowledge out of people through verbal exchange. In a similar fashion, in the elicitive model of dialogue and dialogue training, the idea is that the dialogue

36 John Paul Lederach, *Preparing for Peace: Conflict Transformation across Cultures* (Syracuse, NY: Syracuse University Press, 1995), 31.

group itself, or those involved with the encounter, not only elicit the wisdom, knowledge, and resources necessary to create together (co-create) the ground rules, goals, and facilitation parameters for the encounter but also ultimately hold much of the truth, wisdom, and skills necessary to achieve the intended outcomes. It is certainly a best practice to establish ground rules prior to any potentially difficult dialogue or encounter. Ground rules may be either preset beforehand or elicited from the group in a co-creative process; however, with either approach, participants ought to be invited in to change, revise, or reject any ground rules. After all, *rules are for fools*, and "people are more likely to follow agreements they helped to create."[37]

37 Mohamed Abu-Nimer, Anas Alabbadi, and Cynthia Marquez, *Building Bridges: Guide for Dialogue Ambassadors* (Kuala Lumpur: World Organization of the Scout Movement and Vienna: International Dialogue Centre, 2018), 9.

Nonviolent Communication

The well-known method of compassionate or Nonviolent Communication (NVC) developed by Marshall Rosenberg has emerged to be among the most flexible and "shovel-ready" techniques of dialogue today, useful from intimate two-person parent-child or husband-wife communication to massive multistate high-level international peacekeeping processes. Simple in theory and easy to deploy, yet difficult to perfect in practice, NVC rests on the premise that conflict most often arises when one or more individuals' needs are not being met and the principle that "creating a connection between the people who are in conflict is the most important thing."[38] The NVC process invites practitioners to humanize the other, avoid labels, and enter into a compassionate method of negotiating conflict by following four basic steps:

---

38 Marshall B. Rosenberg, *Nonviolent Communication: A Language of Life*, 3rd ed. (Encinitas, CA: Puddle Dancer Press, 2015), 161.

ESTABLISH GROUND RULES

Common basic ground rules might include the following:

- Listen openly, actively, and without interruption in order to understand others rather than thinking of how to defend your own views.
- Make requests, not demands.
- Respect others, avoid name-calling, and do not try to persuade or change others.
- Speak in the first person from personal experience rather than assuming experiences of others or speaking on behalf of a group. Likewise, avoid ascribing views to others that they do not ascribe to themselves.
- Try to minimize external disruptions.
- Honor confidentiality. What is said in the group stays in the group.
- Ask questions from a place of empathetic curiosity.

- Remain committed through challenging times.
- Aim for understanding and clarity, not agreement.
- Acknowledge common ground when possible while respecting differences.
- If offended, avoid disengaging and instead communicate that you have been offended so that others might grow.
- Compare your own ideals with the ideals of the conversation partner and your own practices with their practices.
- Accept and make room for feelings.
- Avoid side conversations with others (for a virtual video chat environment, this might mean avoid using the text chat function).[1]

---

1 This list of ground rules draws on Lisa Schirch and David Campt, *The Little Book of Dialogue for Difficult Subjects: A Practical, Hands-On Guide* (New York: Good Books, 2007), 40–41; Bryn et al., "What Is Dialogue?", 16–17; and Abu-Nimer et al., *Building Bridges*, 8.

1) Begin with a clear statement or ***observation*** of a concrete action that affects our well-being: "When I see our community center being used for religious activities that I do not recognize as part of my own tradition . . ."
2) Followed by a ***feeling*** in relation to the observation: "I feel anxious and like I do not belong."
3) Followed by an explanation of ***needs*** or values: ". . . because I value a sense of community, belonging, and harmony in our shared spaces."
4) Ending with a ***request***: "Would you be willing to discuss various ways we might ensure fair use of our community center that may meet all of our needs?"

"Founded on the language and communication skills that strengthen our ability to remain human, even under trying conditions," Rosenberg admits, NVC "contains nothing new; all that has been integrated into NVC has been known for centuries."[39] Many people are raised in cultures, families, and societies that teach (whether explicitly or implicitly) a method of conflict response based on instinctual judgment and blaming language (e.g., "Why didn't you clean your room? You're so lazy!"). NVC, on the other hand, "guides us in reframing how we express ourselves and hear others. Instead of habitual, automatic responses, our words become conscious responses based firmly on awareness of what we are perceiving, feeling, and wanting."[40] Not only do we more readily understand the deep needs of those with whom we engage, but also "we come to hear our own deeper needs . . . NVC trains us to observe carefully, and to be able to specify behaviors and conditions that are affecting us. We learn to identify and clearly articulate what we are concretely wanting in any given situation. The form is simple, but powerfully transformative."[41] One of the most

---

39 Rosenberg, *Nonviolent Communication*, 3.
40 Rosenberg, *Nonviolent Communication*, 3.
41 Rosenberg, *Nonviolent Communication*, 3.

common human needs is wanting to be heard, acknowledged, and valued; hence, sometimes (perhaps even often) human connection can be established, and conflicts solved, as simply as actively acknowledging others. The three simple words "I hear you"[42] can hold remarkable power.

One should be graceful, respectful, and charitable with those they engage, not only by actively listening and acknowledging them but also by considering letting them be wrong sometimes, honoring the reality that we all make mistakes and are sometimes wrong. Sometimes dialogue partners are flat-out wrong, oversimplify, and make mistakes. Everyone does this. Sometimes it is appropriate to let others be wrong,[43] especially if it has little bearing on the topic at hand.

---

42 Among eleven best practices to improve listening skills, Peter Boghossian and James Lindsay include "say, 'I hear you,' to acknowledge you're listening. Mean it. 'I hear you' is simple yet effective" (Peter Boghossian and James Lindsay, *How to Have Difficult Conversations: A Very Practical Guide* [New York: Hachette, 2019], 22).

43 See "Let Friends Be Wrong," in Boghossian and Lindsay, *How to Have Difficult Conversations*, 73–76.

Acknowledge Asymmetry and Aspire to Symmetry

Although "good dialogue requires not similar, but equal partners"[44] or, as Iranian-American Islamic scholar and philosopher Seyyed Hossein Nasr claims, "dialogue is possible only among equals or those nearly equal,"[45] the reality is that dialogue "is always contextualized by power. . . . in which difference between individuals is not simply cultural but also recognizably unequal. At any moment, one person or the other is always more knowing or more vulnerable or more powerful."[46] In short, a healthy encounter strives to create symmetrical relations among participants while simultaneously acknowledging the unequal or asymmetrical relations that

---

44 Bryn et al., "What Is Dialogue?" 16.

45 Seyyed Hossein Nasr, *The Need for a Sacred Science* (Albany: SUNY Press, 1993), 166; cited in Frances Sleap and Omer Sener, *Dialogue Theories*, ed. Paul Weller (London: Dialogue Society, 2013), 144.

46 Michael Atkinson, "Paulo Freire," in *Dialogue Theories*, vol. 2, ed. Omer Sener, Frances Sleap, and Paul Weller (London: Dialogue Society, 2016), 128.

are present. The "assumption of symmetry" from the outset is identified by human rights attorney Jonathan Kuttab as one of the most common "pitfalls of dialogue."[47] Levinas recognized this inherent asymmetrical nature of human relations. Furthermore, Levinas claims that in dialogue there exists a degree of "self-sacrifice, or an 'asymmetry' between what I give up and what I receive in return."[48] Such asymmetry, not only among participants prior to the encounter but also in the give-and-take of the encounter itself, in which "the self is truly open to the Other," can shake the very "foundations of the self's identity."[49] This is because, for Levinas, the very foundation of dialogue rests on "a response to the Other, who calls the self to responsibility."[50] Dialogue is thus understood as a fundamental

---

47 Green, *Peacebuilding in Divided Communities*, 98.

48 Andrew Wilshere, "Emmanuel Levinas," in *Dialogue Theories*, vol. 2, ed. Omer Sener, Frances Sleap, and Paul Weller (London: Dialogue Society, 2016), 198.

49 Wilshere, "Emmanuel Levinas," 198.

50 Wilshere, "Emmanuel Levinas," 198.

human orientation or attitude of being responsible to and for others. For Levinas, according to British philosopher Andrew Wilshere, "It is the presence of the Other that brings first-person consciousness into existence and makes experience and selfhood possible."[51] In other words, Levinas's understanding of dialogue resonates with the concept of *ubuntu*, a Zulu word from South Africa that emphasizes not only humanity but also the radical and ontological interdependence of humanity. It is commonly translated to express the idea that "I am because you are." In other words, the *being* of human beings—their very ontological existence—depends on one another. In short, individuals become human through other humans.[52] *Ubuntu* informs conflict mediation by emphasizing the radical interdependence of humanity and the restoration of

51 Wilshere, "Emmanuel Levinas," 191.

52 Kimberly Vrudny, "Artists as Prophets and Visionaries: An Ubuntu-Inspired Renewal of Christianity," in *Between Shadow and the Light*, ed. Rachel Hostetter Smith (Grand Rapids, MI: Calvin College, 2014), 33.

broken relationships. Thich Nhật Hanh, the well-known twentieth-century Vietnamese Buddhist monk, maintains a similar concept he refers to as "interbeing" to convey the idea that "I am, therefore you are. You are therefore, I am . . . We inter-are."[53] Needless to say, Levinas, *ubuntu*, and interbeing all impart that deeply profound claim that being truly and authentically human is bound up in relation to others, and dialogue serves as the response or attitude toward that orientation. Wilshere suggests, "We could summarize Levinas' core phenomenological argument as follows: *the relation of responsibility-for-the-Other is what makes first-person experience of a meaningful world possible.*"[54] The challenge for the group, the facilitator, or individuals in an encounter is to seek equality without ignoring

53 Thich Nhật Hanh, *Being Peace* (Berkeley: Paralax Press, 1987), 87; cited in Matthew Maruggi, "Disorienting Solidarity: Engaging Difference and Developing 'Fluidarity,'" *Journal of Interreligious Studies* 31 (2020): 40.

54 Wilshere, "Emmanuel Levinas," 192; *emphasis* original.

how "power dynamics can harm and affect the openness."[55]

Empathetic Curiosity

After attempting to walk a mile in another person's shoes and realizing that it's not possible to fully walk a mile in their shoes, that their shoes won't fit, or that they simply cannot experience it as the other person does, one should consider embracing empathic curiosity and asking questions to gain an understanding of what it might be like to walk a mile in their shoes. Lieutenant Jack Cambria, former chief hostage negotiator for the New York City Police Department, emphasizes the importance of empathy in tense and potential conflict situations. Cambria teaches that negotiators must "experience the emotion of love at one point in their life, to know what it means to have been hurt in love at one point in their life, to know success and perhaps, most important, to know what it means to know

---

55 Abu-Nimer et al., *Building Bridges*, 73.

failure."[56] This understanding of empathy is a crucial tool for understanding others in real-world scenarios.

Psychology professor Stuart Kirschner, co-creator with Cambria of a hostage negotiation training program, reports that Cambria operates out of a place of empathy: "The (training) sessions that we had are incredibly moving, because he taps into their own experience. It's almost like group therapy. . . . He puts psychologists to shame with what he does."[57] In perhaps one of the most intense scenarios imaginable—a hostage negotiation—the skill to demonstrate empathy emerges as a top tactic to lower the temperature, make human connection, and build trust. Imagine what empathy might accomplish in less tense, more ordinary everyday moments

---

56 Pervaiz Shallwani, "Life Lessons from the NYPD's Top Hostage Negotiator," *Wall Street Journal*, August 29, 2015, https://www.wsj.com/articles/life-lessons-from-the-nypds-top-hostage-negotiator-1440726792.

57 Shallwani, "Life Lessons."

of interreligious and inter-ideological encounter and misunderstanding.

Scholar of interreligious dialogue Catherine Cornille identifies empathy as the "ability to resonate with the beliefs and practices of the other [, which] helps to break down barriers, while the inability to do so tends to cast the religious other as strange and threatening. Empathy may be located somewhere on the border between knowledge and skill. It involves experiential knowledge of the other that may be more innate as a personal skill in some, while requiring more effort in others."[58] A basic exercise in empathy asks the individual to "put yourself in the place of the person in front of you to understand and feel what the other person is experiencing from his/her own perspective. In other words, try to see the situation as they see it. What does it mean for them? How does it feel? This is an important skill and competence everyone needs to develop

58 Catherine Cornille, "Interreligious Empathy," in *Interreligious Studies*, ed. Hans Gustafson (Waco, TX: Baylor University Press, 2020), 223.

and eventually master through dialogue."[59] Thus, while empathy is a universal skill to be cultivated, its application, as illustrated by the insights of Cambria and Cornille, takes on unique dimensions in various encounters.

A key component of empathy, as demonstrated by Cambria, is that it does not require individuals to have exactly the same experiences, nor does it necessarily entail having walked a mile in another's shoes. In the context of encounter across religious difference, "interreligious empathy does not involve duplicating the experience of the other," Cornille teaches; rather, "any resonance with the religious life of the other will be colored by one's own religious background, experiences, and dispositions."[60] Building on this understanding of empathy in interreligious settings, the approach extends to broader aspects of dialogue and leadership, as emphasized by the Nansen Center, where empathy becomes a

59 Abu-Nimer et al., *Building Bridges*, 46.
60 Cornille, "Interreligious Empathy," 226.

foundational tool for deeper understanding and connection.

For effective dialogue (and leadership), the Nansen Center for Peace and Dialogue stresses the "need for empathy to understand another person properly. Empathy can be learned by becoming aware of one's own need for understanding. Empathic curiosity is at the core of a dialogue process."[61] Curiosity for the sake of empathy refers to the will and ability to ask questions that allow an individual to gain insights, to the degree that it is possible, to resonate with the experiences, beliefs, and practices of others—not only for greater understanding of the other but for greater self-understanding and self-awareness as well.

Be Open to Change

I won't retire but I might retread,[62] utters the fictional character Grandpa, sitting on his porch,

61 Grande and Seehausen, eds., *The Nansen Handbook*, 27.

62 Neil Young and Crazy Horse, "Falling from Above," track 1 on *Greendale*, Warner Bros., 2003, compact disc.

in the opening lyrics to the first track on Neil Young's *Greendale* album. A basic wisdom can be gleaned: no matter how old or stuck in one's ways an individual is, that person can always be willing to change, transform, shift gears, and consider novel approaches. In the context of dialogue, consider both suggestions: 1) don't retire but 2) retread. While the former calls for commitment, the latter beckons an individual to be open to change.

Bryn and colleagues teach that while dialogue involves gaining insight into one's own culture as one among many, and adopting the attitude of patiently striving to better understand others, it also calls for not abandoning what one holds to be true and right, unless persuaded by strong reasons to do so.[63] This reinforces Diana Eck's mantra, which preaches "the new paradigm of pluralism does not require us to leave our identities and our commitments

63 Bryn et al., "What Is Dialogue?" 10.

behind, for pluralism is the encounter of commitments. It means holding our deepest differences, even our religious differences, not in isolation, but relation to one another."[64] While practitioners and scholars call for commitment on the one hand, they often proclaim the necessity of being open to change even more so on the other hand.

Echoing this concept of transformation through dialogue, Anne Hege Grung, Norwegian scholar of interreligious studies, highlights the importance of mutual change among participants, aligning closely with Gadamer's perspective on creating a "third culture" through dialogue. Grung emphasizes the element of *mutual* change among dialogue participants: "One is not entering a dialogue with the aim of transforming the other(s), but to take part in the possible mutual transformation which might

64 "What Is Pluralism?"

be the result of the encounter."[65] Recall Hans-Georg Gadamer's vision of dialogue includes an opportunity for participants to generate a "third culture" by entering into a process of dialogue that challenges one's preconceived "prejudices" (which are not necessarily negative but can simply provide the foundation on which one builds knowledge[66]) and thus opens the opportunity for challenge, change, and new insights.

In short, the principle of "expect to be changed"[67] ought to be included on any short list of top principles for dialogue. As a bridge- and peacebuilding tool, dialogue "is transformative

---

65 Anne Hege Grung, "Including Gender Perspective in Muslim-Christian Dialogue in Europe and Scandinavia—A Disturbance to Bridge-building or a Contextual Necessity?" In *Mission to the World: Communicating the Gospel in the 21st Century: Essays in Honor of Knud Jørgensen*, ed. Tormod Engelsviken, Ernst Harbakk, Rolv Olsen, and Thor Strandenaes (Eugene, OR: Wipf and Stock, 2009), 290; cited in Oddbjørn Leirvik, "Philosophies of Interreligious Dialogue," *Approaching Religion* 1, no. 1 (2011): 21–22.

66 Paul Hedges, *Understanding Religion* (Oakland: University of California Press, 2021), 53.

67 Abu-Nimer et al., *Building Bridges*, 86, 89.

because it changes the individual perception of the other and therefore of the conflict. When these changes are mutual, the dialogue transforms the relations between the parties from adversarial to respectful, opening the way to create new relationships."[68] Dialogue is not just an exchange of ideas but also a transformative interaction that reshapes perspectives and relationships while fostering a culture of respect and novel insights.

Imagination

Some dialogue scholars and practitioners argue that finding a perfectly synchronized and commensurable language for interreligious dialogue is impossible—that is, no common language exists that allows for perfect one-to-one translation between religious and spiritual worldviews. For instance, when a Christian and a Buddhist talk about compassion in their respective traditions, it is likely their concepts of compassion are

---

68 Abu-Nimer et al., *Building Bridges*, 21.

different (i.e., they are incommensurable). Given that interreligious dialogue often emphasizes "commonalities between religions,"[69] the issue of incommensurability becomes increasingly important because it strengthens the skeptic's argument that questions both the impact and feasibility of such dialogue.

Marianne Moyaert proposes one path out of this conundrum by looking to insights from intercultural philosophy and intercultural communication, which teach that although "diversity cannot be encompassed in a common framework, . . . this does not put an end to dialogue."[70] To overcome this potential impasse, Moyaert proposes the utilization of the human capacity to imagine: "Imagination allows people to locate differences and equivalences and question static and essentialized interpretations of religious languages. Imagination is the human capacity

69 Marianne Moyaert, "Interreligious Dialogue and the Debate between Universalism and Particularism," *Studies in Interreligious Dialogue* 15, no. 1 (2005): 37.

70 Moyaert, "Interreligious Dialogue," 48.

that makes empathy possible and enables us to cross boundaries and to enter different worlds and perspective."[71] Many religious and cultural traditions themselves preserve and communicate their core insights through narrative, story, and ritual and not theory or abstract principles. Likewise, Moyaert endorses the power of story and narrative for constructive interreligious encounter since it allows "people to recognize themselves in or to identify themselves with one of the characters. Stories provide topics of conversation and succeed in bringing about a real dialogue. Stories create our imagination and it is this capacity that makes empathy and a 'crossing over' possible. Interreligious dialogue is the place where we can listen to the stories of religious others and enter their world."[72] Hence, this final insight imparts the instruction to maintain faith in the human capacity for imagination and its ability to cultivate empathy in the face of others' stories.

---

71 Moyaert, "Interreligious Dialogue," 48.
72 Moyaert, "Interreligious Dialogue," 49.

* * *

Practical communication requires a balance between structure and flexibility. Effective dialogue requires a blend of foundational principles and adaptability to specific contexts and needs. The range of guidelines introduced in this chapter serve as tools rather than rigid rules. Spirited, life-giving dialogue is found not in strict adherence to rules but in the ability to respond dynamically to the encounter, always with an eye to fostering understanding, growth, and transformative connection.

CHAPTER FOUR

Proverbial Wisdom for Encounter

This chapter introduces proverbial wisdom for enhancing everyday human interactions by exploring how adopting certain principles can aid in transforming negative dynamics into positive connections across various religious, cultural, and ideological contexts. The proverbs emphasize the importance of setting aside preconceived notions to authentically engage with others to create environments conducive to constructive human connection. The chapter introduces insights from *Improv Wisdom* and specific proverbs that encapsulate nonjudgment, kindness, forgiveness, dialogue, resilience, and excellence. They are "drop the story," "just kill them with kindness," "give them a third chance," "dialogue is a useful imperfect tool," "got sisu?", and "be excellent to each other." These proverbs collectively offer guidance on transforming poisonous conversations into peaceful, everyday human dialogue.

INSIGHTS FROM *IMPROV WISDOM*

Patricia Ryan Madson spent four decades teaching drama at Stanford University. Among her many accomplishments is the publication of a short book[1] that provides life lessons from the

---

1 Patricia Ryan Madson, *Improv Wisdom: Don't Prepare, Just Show Up* (New York: Bell Tower, 2005).

world of improv. She teaches thirteen maxims that apply to improv and life, but they also readily and remarkably apply to interreligious dialogue and leadership.

Say Yes

This guideline preaches an attitude that embraces courage, optimism, and a positive can-do orientation to people, problems, and encounters. It strives to say yes to new situations, new challenges, new questions, and new opportunities. Not only does it ask the participant to seek the sunny side of issues without losing sight of the shadows, but above all it also asks individuals to say yes to seeking what is right and true. It encourages responses such as "I'm with you," "I hear you," "good idea," and "you are right" and actively strives to replace "yes, *but* . . ." with "yes, *and*. . ."[2] An overarching goal of the "say yes" guideline is to build optimism and hope in search of authentic connection.

---

2 Madson, *Improv Wisdom*, 34.

Show Up

The well-known colloquialism, often attributed to Woody Allen, preaches that X percent of success in life is just showing up, with X ranging anywhere from 10 to 90 percent but generally toward the higher end. Simply being present can make all the difference in the world, regardless of an individual's level of response or engagement. In contexts of dialogue and encounter, half the challenge is often just showing up or making the commitment to being present. Dialogue does not require that people agree with those they encounter. Rather, as Diana Eck teaches, it involves "the commitment to being at the table—with one's commitments."[3] Showing up and being present at the table of dialogue signal an individual's openness to being with and serving the needs of others. Madson's eighth maxim preaches to "stay the course" and reminds us "there is meaning in everything we do, even the small tasks. [And thus, you ought to] keep an eye

3 "What Is Pluralism?" The Pluralism Project, accessed April 1, 2021, https://pluralism.org/about.

on where you are going."[4] In other words, show up, stay committed, and focus on being present.

Attend to the Immediate

Attending to the immediate is another way of pointing to the value of being present in the moment of an encounter. Resonating with Anna Katharina Schaffner's tenth "timeless truth" of self-improvement, "be present,"[5] Madson's second maxim of Improv Wisdom teaches "don't prepare." If an individual is preoccupied with concerns from their immediate past (what happened that morning or yesterday) or future (what they need to accomplish later that day or prior to going to bed), they are more likely to miss out on the conversation or encounter immediately before them. Madson wisely preaches to "attend carefully to what is happening right now; allow

---

4 Madson, *Improv Wisdom*, 88.

5 Anna Katharina Schaffner, *The Art of Self-Improvement* (New Haven, CT: Yale University Press, 2021).

yourself to be surprised,"[6] for if one is constantly preoccupied with concerns not in the present, one is probably not actively listening. "The will to listen to the other" remains an absolute bedrock prerequisite for any successful encounter or dialogue across difference.[7]

Embrace Imperfection

Embracing imperfection corresponds to Madson's fifth maxim to "be average." It suggests a healthier climate is likely created when participants let go and acknowledge their own and other's imperfections. Instead of striving for constant perfection, uniqueness, and attention-seeking innovation and insight, Madson counsels practitioners that "close enough is perfect. Dare to be dull. . . . Celebrate the obvious. [Remember that] what is ordinary for you is often a revelation

---

6 Madson, *Improv Wisdom*, 44.

7 Norunn Grande and Christiane Seehausen, eds., *The Nansen Handbook for Trainers in Dialogue and Conflict Transformation* (Lillehammer: Nansen Fredssenter, 2018), 20.

to others."[8] Showing up with an inward anxiety about constantly driving new innovative ideas, solutions, and insights can often backfire and result in showing up in contrived unrealistic, unauthentic, and often uncomfortable ways (for ourselves and others). Letting go and embracing one's imperfection can alleviate this anxiety and result in a more authentic and inviting self in such encounters. Madson ends her explanation of this maxim with the terse command "Don't make jokes. Make sense."[9]

Be Other-Centered

"Become a detective. Shift your attention from yourself to others. Make an effort to remember names and faces."[10] It sounds simple, but it is not always so easy. The Nansen Center's *Handbook for Trainers in Dialogue and Conflict Transformation* claims that "empathetic curiosity is at

8 Madson, *Improv Wisdom*, 66.
9 Madson, *Improv Wisdom*, 66.
10 Madson, *Improv Wisdom*, 76.

the core of a dialogue process."[11] Empathetic curiosity is radically other-centered in its seeking to know the needs, feelings, and experiences of others as they experience them, to the extent possible. Likewise, in such encounters, the person demonstrating empathetic curiosity—asking about the needs, feelings, and experiences of the other—often discovers their own capacity for empathizing and their own desire for others to understand their needs, feelings, and experiences.

Accept People as They Are

Madson's seventh maxim is "face the facts," which culminates with the practical advice to "accept other people as they are. Work with what you have been given. . . . Insecurity is normal. Count on it."[12] Another variation on the themes of humanizing, avoiding essentializing, and

11 Grande and Seehausen, eds., *The Nansen Handbook*, 27.

12 Madson, *Improv Wisdom*, 83.

looking beyond the group identities of an individual, the wisdom here is that the act of embracing the imperfect messiness of life and of others can bring the world to life. As Madson phrases it, "In the act of balancing, we come alive."[13] People tend to hyper-focus on what is directly in front of them, work with the resources available in the room, and accept both themselves and others, limitations and all. In navigating this inherent messiness, they often encounter the realities of living, thereby becoming more prepared to respond to both life's challenges and the needs of others.

Savor the Details

Madson's decade of experience taught her "There is always something there to work with; you just need to see it,"[14] which forms the basis of her ninth maxim to "wake up to the gifts." This maxim also points to the value of finding,

13 Madson, *Improv Wisdom*, 82.
14 Madson, *Improv Wisdom*, 89.

savoring, and treasuring the details that already exist in the people, traditions, and experiences in the room, no matter how small or insignificant they seem. After all, people are complicated, and when the details of their uniqueness emerge and are acknowledged, they become humanized and set apart from any shared elements of identity they might have. Not only is waking up to the gifts among the people in the room a wise maxim; it also opens the possibility to a basic teaching of Paulo Freire that first and foremost "dialogue is guided by the experiences of participants."[15] It recalls the principle from asset-based community development, inspired by Freire's work, that "assumes local people are experts with regards to their own development."[16] To put it colloquially, the principle teaches what Bill Murray's character Phil Connors learned over an unknown number of lifetimes in the

---

15 Michael Atkinson, "Paulo Freire," in *Dialogue Theories*, vol. 2, ed. Omer Sener, Frances Sleap, and Paul Weller (London: Dialogue Society, 2016), 127.

16 Atkinson, "Paulo Freire," 133.

classic 1993 film *Groundhog Day*: everything he needed to flourish, be happy, and live well was already at hand in Punxsutawney, where he exclaims at the end of the film, "It's so beautiful! Let's live here."

"Make Mistakes, Please"

This phrase guides Madson's tenth maxim. The reality of making mistakes is part of what it means to be human. Furthermore, being open to mistakes raises an individual's tolerance to risk and self-challenge. Madson teaches her improv students to "let go of outcomes. Cultivate a flexible mind. Mistakes may actually be blessings."[17] Nansen Center faculty observes, "When people meet face to face in a safe setting, something always happens."[18] In the context of interreligious encounter, Kate McCarthy

17 Madson, *Improv Wisdom*, 113.

18 Steinar Bryn, Inge Edisvåg, and Ingunn Skurdall, "What Is Dialogue?" in *Understanding the Other: Dialogue as a Tool and an Attitude to Life* (Lillehammer: Nansen Fredssenter, 2015), 13.

similarly recognizes, "Interfaith encounters are always encounters between people, and therefore unpredictable."[19] Though the outcomes of a particular encounter or dialogue remain uncertain, something always happens—often differing from the original plan—and sometimes, perhaps often, the unintended consequences exceed the intended consequences, especially when those involved remain committed to listening to and humanizing others in ways that engender safe risk-taking and mistake-making.

Give Yourself Away

Madson's twelfth maxim, "take care of each other," is perhaps the most aspirational of the maxims as it strives for an almost idyllic level of friendship as it rests on the foundation of cultivating compassion for people we encounter. She advises, "Sometimes the only thing we can do is to join the suffering of others—to be

---

19 Kate McCarthy, *Interfaith Encounters in America* (New Brunswick, NJ: Rutgers University Press, 2007), 18.

there alongside them. There is no fix, no remedy. But we dare not leave our comrade alone in distress."[20] We needn't become deep friends with all those we encounter, nor do we need to always engage them in deep dialogue; that needn't be the goal, nor is it possible or a realistic expectation. It is a welcome unintended consequence.

"DROP THE STORY"

Mark T. Unno, scholar in East Asian religions and Japanese Buddhism, recounts a personal story from 2009 about serving on a search committee for the University of Oregon to hire an assistant director for their Center for Intercultural Dialogue. During the interview process, they asked all the candidates, "For working in an intercultural context, what skill do you consider to be the most important?" One of the most memorable responses came from a candidate who simply replied, "Drop the story." Unno recalls,

---

20 Madson, *Improv Wisdom*, 123–24.

At first, I was not sure if what I heard was correct, so I asked her to repeat her answer, and again she said, "Drop the story." "What do you mean by that? Can you explain?" "In my previous work, whenever I was sent abroad, I would do prior research on the people and their culture. Yet, I eventually learned that, once having arrived *in situ*, I had to drop whatever story had formed in my mind about who I thought these people were or should be according to my expectations. Only by "dropping the story" I had formed of them, could I actually encounter who they were as living human beings. It's not that the research I had done prior to my visit was useless, but I could not let my book learning lead my expectations for the visit. Rather, I could make use of that knowledge as supporting and informing the more immediate experience of meeting people in the moment of encounter."[21]

---

21 Mark Unno, "Buddhist-Christian Dialogue: Mystery of the Naked Heart," *Buddhist-Christian Studies* 40 (2020): 309.

"Drop the story" is the only response Unno remembers from that hiring round, and he highlights how this powerful, simple suggestion prompts reflection on the extent to which one is aware of the assumptions they bring to any human encounter. He raises the question: to what degree is it truly possible to "drop the story" in the first place? Furthermore, Unno asks, "What does it really mean to 'encounter the other,' to engage in dialogue, to form relationships: interreligious, intercultural, interhuman? In Japanese, there is an expression, '*Sode fure au mo tashō no en nari.*' Roughly translated, this means, 'Even kimono sleeves brushing past each other is the result of innumerable karmic factors coalescing in the moment.'"[22] Unno suggests that every interaction, no matter how fleeting, has the potential to influence, alter, and potentially transform us, underscoring the importance of carefully observing those we

22 Unno, "Buddhist-Christian Dialogue," 309.

meet and understanding ourselves through the perspectives of others.[23]

The proverb "drop the story" serves as a vital reminder for engaging in healthy human dialogue across differences by emphasizing the need to approach each encounter with a spirit of humility and open-mindedness. By setting aside preconceived notions and embracing the unpredictable nature of human interactions, one opens oneself to genuine understanding and connection, fostering environments where diversity is not just recognized but also engaged, welcomed, and appreciated. As Unno teaches, "In encountering the religious Other, I need to try to 'drop the story' so that I can see the Other."[24] This approach not only holds the potential to enrich personal experiences but can also strengthen the fabric of societies.

"JUST KILL THEM WITH KINDNESS"

"Just kill them with kindness," preached the restaurant general manager every night to all

23 Unno, "Buddhist-Christian Dialogue," 309–10.
24 Unno, "Buddhist-Christian Dialogue," 311.

the table servers. As all those working with the general public in customer service know, not all customers are pleasant, especially when they are not served in a timely or satisfactory manner. The general manager advocated for the practice of standing firm in the face of an onslaught of insults and dissatisfaction, assuring customers that they are heard and taken seriously and that responses are always laced with kindness. Most of the time, the customer calms down and apologizes, often embarrassed at their outburst over mostly trivial matters. A table server losing patience and responding to a customer with an in-kind aggressive, unkind demeanor generally only prolongs and escalates the conflict, exacerbating the misunderstanding. So best just to weather the storm and *kill them with kindness.* This pithy and powerful quip can be understood both positively and negatively. The thrust of it is to bombard the other with overwhelming kindness. However, if done carelessly or lacking foresight, such unbridled kindness can be counterproductive and end up harming the other in the long term and perhaps even literally kill, hence the literal interpretation *to kill with kindness.*

On the other hand, it seems, the saying is increasingly understood with the positive connotation to refer to an attitude of donning the weaponry of kindness in a mission to win over the other as a friend no matter how unpleasant they are in return or how long it takes. It is not easy and often calls one to lose their pride in the moment. Recall Panikkar's teaching that "the way to encounter the other is to listen to him, and the way to listen to him without misunderstanding him is to love him, and the way to love him is to be free from my egoistic pride."[25] Killing them with kindness might be

25 Raimon Panikkar, "Toward a Theory of Intercultural and Interreligious Liberation," in *Opera Omnia, Vol. 6: Cultures and Religions in Dialogue, Part One: Pluralism and Interculturality*, ed. Milena Carrara Pavan (Maryknoll, NY: Orbis Books, 2018), 143; first published as "Hacia una Teología de la Liberación," in *Interculturalidad, Diálogo y Liberación*, ed. H. Küng, J. J. Tamayo-Acosta, and R. Forneet-Betancourt (Pamplona: Verbo Divini, 2005), 61–68.

the unwavering commitment to battle through the slings and arrows of insults, slights, and disrespect to not allow the other to move you to hate but to ultimately bring the other over to your side as a friend. Eboo Patel, demonstrating his admiration of the Tibetan Buddhist monks who during the Free Tibet movement were concerned they'd lose love and compassion for their captors who treated them harshly and hatefully, reflects, "One of the lessons that I learned in reading the work of Buddhist monks who were involved in the Free Tibet movement is that perhaps you don't respond to your opponent in kind, you don't let their hate or anger drive your behavior. You are anchored somewhere else."[26] Such sentiment captures the aim of this proverb to convert the toxins of hate into a vibrant array of kindness. Certainly, there are limits to and concerns with such an approach. One may end

26 Eboo Patel, "Bridges of Cooperation: Interfaith Action toward Racial Equity," webinar from College of Saint Benedict, St. Joseph, Minnesota, November 20, 2020, 00:14:34–53; https://www.youtube.com/live/RiiPKKkGo08?feature=shared.

up doing more harm than good to the other and to themselves if not properly carried out and monitored.

The aforementioned Daryl Davis, featured in the 2016 documentary film *Accidental Courtesy: Daryl Davis, Race, and America*, is a Black American musician and racial reconciliation expert who controversially befriends white supremacist Ku Klux Klan members and convinces them to disavow their once-held racist ideologies. Davis approaches these individuals not with respect for or acceptance of their racist ideologies but with respect for their dignity as a human person like himself. He treats them as humans by listening to them and respecting them without agreeing with them. Over time, Davis wears them down with courtesy and kindness as they slowly shed their racist worldviews and become close friends with him. Akin to the way many Black South Africans drew on the concept of *ubuntu* to love white South Africans into humanity, into existence, and out of their racism, Davis loves these white supremacist Americans out of their hate-ridden racism.

Although Davis doesn't necessarily kill them with kindness, he kills their internal racist worldviews by treating them as humans with courtesy and respect. This is no small feat and is certainly not a skill that comes easily for most. In dialogue and encounter, people may come face to face with ideas, worldviews, and concepts that demonize, hate, misrepresent, mistreat, and disrespect them. If the environment maintains certain conditions (safety, trust, opportunities for brave resiliency, etc.), the proverb *kill them with kindness* can, over time, prove a successful long-term strategy. However, if certain conditions are not present, such an approach can be more harmful than beneficial, to all parties involved. Not everyone has the initial capacity to confront hate directly like Daryl Davis or the resurrected Christ figure in Dostoevsky's *The Grand Inquisitor*, but many can identify and seize opportunities, regardless of their size, to acknowledge our shared humanity and overcome hatred with kindness.

GIVE THEM A THIRD CHANCE?

The idea is rather simple: Do not give up on anyone right away. Allow others to make mistakes. Years ago, during a television broadcast of an American football game, after one of the offensive players made a remarkable play, one of commentators quickly pointed out how this player had struggled to remain on a team due to personal "off the field" incidents and recounted a story of a previous teammate's response when asked whether any team should give this guy a chance. The teammate's response, paraphrased from memory, was something along the lines of, "Hell yes, you should give him a second chance. You should then give him a third and fourth chance. We all struggle and mess up in life—every one of us, if we're honest—but we're all human and trying hard."

In dialogue and encounter, one's first attempt or response to something need not be one's last.

They can always change, learn, and grow. Not only do most people likely want others to allow them space to mess up and grow, but they can also extend this underserved gift to others. After all, if one is honest, they will recognize their imperfection and, in spaces of constructive encounter, can work toward more authentic understanding and learning. If people are not allowed to fall down once in a while, they may become too focused on staying upright and perfect. As with most things, such an approach (whether it be in athletics, activities, conversation, etc.) generally leads to stilted and rigid inauthenticity in action and speech, ultimately proving counterproductive for learning, connecting, and understanding across difference.

DIALOGUE IS A USEFUL IMPERFECT TOOL

This book touts dialogue as a constructive tool to be utilized to build relations, understanding, and learning and to work toward potential transformation and action. Leading dialogue practitioners express caution here with an emphasis on dialogue as a tool—and an imperfect one at that. Tools make tasks easier, more efficient, successful, and sustainable. However, tools do not do the work on their own. A hammer does not build a house apart from the carpenter, from whom time and effort are still required. Likewise, dialogue is not the only tool in the toolbox. It does not replace action. Nor is dialogue a panacea.[27] Paula Green, founder of the Karuna Center for Peacebuilding, teaches, "We are very clear with our participants that dialogue is one among many tools in peacebuilding, and that it is not a panacea or a cure-all for conflict. . . . Dialogue in our eyes is not a substitute for action, but often a useful prelude to actions that confront oppression."[28] In similar

27 Paula Green, *Peacebuilding in Divided Communities: Karuna Center's Approach to Training* (Amherst, MA: Karuna Center for Peacebuilding, 2012), 100; Bryn et al., "What Is Dialogue?" 12.

28 Green, *Peacebuilding in Divided Communities*, 33.

fashion, Steinar Bryn and others at the Nansen Center caution that "Dialogue is no luxury, no pretext for doing nothing. Rather it is the nail mat that forces one to pay attention. . . . Dialogue does not replace negotiations, mediation, truth commissions and litigation. But it is a prerequisite for the success of negotiations and mediation."[29] In short, dialogue is only a first step to the sometimes challenging and difficult action of sustaining the peace, reconciliation, or relationship-building process that prompted the dialogue or encounter in the first place.

GOT *SISU*?

The Upper Peninsula (UP) of Michigan in the United States is home to the highest concentration of Finns outside of Europe and has maintained, to some degree, a Finnish-inspired American way of life all its own with sauna culture, Finnish-language television programming,

29 Bryn et al., "What Is Dialogue?" 13.

and even a Finnish heritage university (Finlandia University). If ever traveling through the raw, rugged, weather-worn landscape of the UP, one may glimpse stickers on vehicles or windows that read "Got Sisu?" Emilia Lahti, a Finnish positive psychologist, explains that *sisu* is a five-hundred-year-old Finnish orientation or way of being, for which there is no direct translation,[30] that relates to "mental toughness and the ability to endure significant stress while taking action against seemingly impossible odds. . . . sisu is a way of life, a philosophy."[31] Lahti's research of *sisu* among Finns and Finnish Americans yielded several understandings of the term. For instance, Finnish media and mainstream narratives occasionally describe *sisu* as "persistence and the

---

30 Lahti suggests the Japanese 頑張る (*ganbaru*) comes the closest, which refers to standing firm or slogging on through challenging times, although the US Navy SEALS' "40% rule" may also come close (see note 37).

31 Emilia Lahti, "Words Make Our Worlds: Introducing Sisu," *The Creativity Post*, June 5, 2014, https://www.creativitypost.com/psychology/words_make_our_worlds_introducing_sisu.

ability to pursue a long-term goal"[32] similar to the popular and recently trendy, yet criticized, professional leadership virtue of perseverance or grit.[33] Lahti discovered the most commonly held view of *sisu* is that it "is a psychological strength capacity enabling individuals to power on when they feel they have reached the limits of their perceived mental or physical capacities."[34] Notice that this is not necessarily the ability to remain persistent or committed to a given task over time. Rather, Lahti argues that *sisu*'s "unique quality is about taking action against the odds and exceeding oneself; going on when there seems to be no way out, and the individual

---

32 Lahti, "Words Make Our Worlds."

33 For example, Angela Duckworth, *Grit: The Power of Passion and Perseverance* (New York: Scribner/Simon and Schuster, 2016); Stephanie Varnon-Hughes, *Interfaith Grit: How Uncertainty Will Save Us* (Eugene, OR: Wipf and Stock, 2018); Marcus Credé, M. C. Tynan, and P. D. Harms, "Much Ado about Grit: A Meta-Analytic Synthesis of the Grit Literature," *Journal of Personality and Social Psychology* 113, no. 3 (2017): 492–511, https://doi.org/10.1037/pspp0000102.

34 Lahti, "Words Make Our Worlds."

is running on empty."[35] Thus, the concept of *sisu* not only highlights a cherished heritage of the UP and Finland but also offers a powerful lens through which to view and navigate the complexities of dialogue and encounter across difference. It offers a potentially profound concept of resilience and determination to move forward, even when challenges appear insurmountable.

This parting proverb to *get sisu* adopts Lahti's clear definition of *sisu* "as part of a broader phenomenon relating to a set of psychological key competencies which enable action to overcome a mentally or physically challenging situation. Sisu is the second wind of mental stamina."[36] Having *sisu* in the context of interreligious dialogue and encounter might refer to adopting an orientation or attitude that assists a group or an individual, having seemingly reached their limits or become exhausted (whether it is due to the process, time, energy, resources, capacity, etc.), to recognize and utilize their deeply rooted

35 Lahti, "Words Make Our Worlds."
36 Lahti, "Words Make Our Worlds."

resilient courage to wield in the face of adversity and stay hopeful amid seemingly impossible circumstances. To put it simply, much like the so-called "40% rule,"[37] it refers to the ability, under safe and appropriate conditions, to not only stay committed and persevere in the dialogue process but also press on when things seem to be at an impasse.

"BE EXCELLENT TO EACH OTHER"

In the 1989 cult-film classic *Bill and Ted's Excellent Adventure*, two teenage boys use a time machine to bring US President Abraham Lincoln into the future of the 1980s to complete

---

37 Popular among Navy SEALS, the elite special operations force of the US Navy, the 40 percent rule refers to when one feels as if their body is totally exhausted. When their mind has reasoned that the body's physical capacity is depleted, all energy is spent, and that they cannot go on, the reality is that their body has only spent 40 percent of its energy. Such a mindset, adopted by US Navy SEALS, assists in pressing on when doing so seems impossible.

their high school history project. Other historical figures include Napoleon Bonaparte, Billy the Kid, Socrates, Sigmund Freud, Ludwig van Beethoven, Genghis Khan, and Joan of Arc. During their schoolwide presentation, President Lincoln recites an updated and revised version of his famous Gettysburg Address, to which he adds "be excellent to each other" as a parting maxim to his audience and an ethical mandate to order one's life by. While this may not qualify as groundbreaking wisdom, the image of a time-traveled Abraham Lincoln to the 1980s Southern California suburbs to declare that people ought to be excellent to each other (and, of course, "party on, dudes!") is certainly more interesting and memorable than generic commandments to "get along and treat each other kindly."

Hence, if one ever loses their way or is at a total loss for direction or for a next move in the context of interreligious dialogue and encounter, then perhaps the 1980s SoCal Abraham Lincoln can be summoned to sit on their shoulder and whisper in their ear, "Be excellent to each other." Such advice, though simple and basic, can go a long way in recentering, and perhaps salvaging, any conversation that has lost its way.

CHAPTER FIVE

Implications of Dialogue

The twentieth-century Tibetan Buddhist teacher Chagdud Tulku eloquently describes the bodhisattva ideal of compassion to alleviate the suffering of all humans regardless of their relation to them, even one's captors and oppressors: "In Tibetan Buddhism, the peacock symbolizes the bodhisattva. A peacock is said to eat poisonous plants, transforming their toxins into the radiant colors of its feathers. It does not poison itself. In the same way, we who advocate peace must not poison ourselves with anger but regard with equanimity those who perpetrate violence, remaining constantly aware of our own state of mind. If we become angry in our efforts, we must pull back and regain our compassionate perspective. Without anger, perhaps we will penetrate the terrible delusion that gives rise to violence and hellish suffering."[1]

Chagdud Tulku recounts a story of a great lama, a respected teacher or spiritual leader, in his family, Tulku Arik, who was imprisoned by the Chinese in 1959 in an effort to clamp down on Tibetan resistance in Tibet. Tulku Arik, elderly and frail, was brutally bound and dragged away when they found him at a spiritual retreat. As he was dragged through the villages, Tibetans recognized him, and to show respect, they came out of their homes to scream

---

1 Chagdud Tulku, compiled and edited by Lama Shenpen Drolma, *Change of Heart: The Bodhisattva Peace Training of Chagdud Tulku* (Junction City, CA: Padma Publishing, 2003), 7.

at and criticize his Chinese captors. Tulku Arik responded to them, "Please, don't worry about me. Help the soldier who is holding this rope. He has blistered his hands dragging me."[2] Once in jail, he was tortured and treated poorly. But Tulku Arik responded to the guards' "ferocity with such gentleness that, by the next day, they began to treat him and the other prisoners more kindly. By being near him, his captors were transformed."[3] This tale of resilience and compassion underlines the transformative power of compassionate engagement, even in the face of adversity, mirroring the way dialogue can turn conflict into opportunities for growth and connection. Just as a peacock consumes poisonous plants and transforms their toxins into vibrant feather colors, dialogue can transform negativity into a vibrant spectrum of positive outcomes that include learning, understanding, peace, and relationships.

---

2 Tulku, *Change of Heart*, 15.

3 Tulku, *Change of Heart*, 15.

ENCOUNTER: TRANSFORMING POISON TO PEACE

"The way to encounter the other is to listen to him, and the way to listen to him without misunderstanding him is to love him, and the way to love him is to be free of my egoistic pride."[4] This guiding principle comes from Raimon Panikkar, a Spanish Roman Catholic priest with three PhDs (philosophy, theology, and chemistry). Everyday human encounter largely involves an individual's willingness to challenge themselves to listen in a manner that removes self-interest and to ardently love and have compassion for the other. Such compassion is exemplified in the bodhisattva ideal of Buddhism to alleviate the suffering of all humans regardless of their

4 Raimon Panikkar, "Toward a Theory of Intercultural and Interreligious Liberation," in *Opera Omnia, Vol. 6: Cultures and Religions in Dialogue, Part One: Pluralism and Interculturality*, ed. Milena Carrara Pavan (Maryknoll, NY: Orbis Books, 2018), 143; first published as "Hacia una Teología de la Liberación," in *Interculturalidad, Diálogo y Liberación*, ed. H. Küng, J. J. Tamayo-Acosta, and R. Forneet-Betancourt (Pamplona: Verbo Divini, 2005), 61–68.

relation to you. This wise recipe for everyday happiness is not a secret, nor is it anything new, for countless religious, cultural, and wisdom traditions (ancient and contemporary) teach that the pursuit of human happiness lies in the personal and social transition from selfishness to selflessness, from self-centeredness to other-centeredness, and in cultivating genuine human connection in community with others in healthy ways. Foundational to authentic human connection is everyday communication and dialogue. Without genuine and constructive communication, the foundational aspects of life people hold most dear—their personal relationships with others and social connections to communities—stand in grave danger of falling apart, perpetuating the growing health crisis referred to as the "epidemic of loneliness and isolation"[5] in the Western world. The profound

5 "Our Epidemic of Loneliness and Isolation: The Surgeon General's Advisory on the Healing Effects of Social Connection and Community," United States Office of the Surgeon General, 2023, https://www.hhs.gov/sites/default/files/surgeon-general-social-connection-advisory.pdf.

implications of radical compassion and the imperative of genuine dialogue have not only shaped historical actions of remarkable figures but also continue to challenge and inspire the broader society to confront its own attitudes toward difference and the reality of suffering.

This ethic of radical compassion was exemplified by Nelson Mandela's move to invite his former prison guards to his presidential inauguration in South Africa and the fourteenth Dalai Lama's reflection in the face of the twentieth century's greatest suffering:

> When I visited the Nazi death camps of Auschwitz, I found myself completely unprepared for the deep revulsion I experienced at the sight of the ovens where hundreds of thousands of human beings were burned. The sheer calculation and detachment to which they bore horrifying witness overcame me. This is what happens, I thought, when societies lose touch with feeling. And while it is necessary to have legislation and international

conventions in place to prevent such disasters, these atrocities happen in spite of them. What of Stalin and his pogroms? What of Pol Pot, architect of the Killing Fields? And what of Mao, a man I knew and once admired, and the barbarous insanity of the Cultural Revolution? All three had a vision, a goal, with some social agenda, but nothing could justify the human suffering engendered. So, you see it all starts with the individual, with asking what the consequences are of your actions. An ethical act is a nonharming act. And if we could enhance our sensitivity to others' suffering, the less we would tolerate seeing others' pain, and the more we would do to ensure that no action of ours ever causes harm. In Tibetan we call this nying je (སྙིང་རྗེ།), translated generally as compassion.[6]

6 Fourteenth Dalai Lama, "On Compassion," interview in Kerry Kennedy, *Speak Truth to Power: Human Rights Defenders Who Are Changing Our World*, ed. Nan Richardson (New York: Umbrage Editions, 2001), 35; Tibetan *uchen* script added.

In Panikkar's guiding principle, Tulku Arik's approach to his captors, Nelson Mandela's selfless reconciliatory approach to peace, and the Dalai Lama's emphasis on the individual, the spirit of radical self-giving kindness and compassion emerges so clearly that it may be perceived as a scandal to the logic and sensibilities of the world of human interaction and encounter. Such scandalization would not be an inappropriate impression, for Panikkar argues that encounter with difference is, as such, "as *subversive* as it is *enriching* and at the same time just as *difficult*. . . . The encounter with other visions of the world that are incompatible with ours make us feel uneasy, insecure, and unbalanced."[7] Everyday encounter can be subversive because deeply

7 Raimon Panikkar, "Peace and Interculturality: A Philosophical Reflection," in *Opera Omnia, Vol. 6: Cultures and Religions in Dialogue*, Part One: Pluralism and Interculturality, ed. Milena Carrara Pavan (Maryknoll, NY: Orbis Books, 2018), 190; *emphasis* original; first published as "Pace e Interculturalitá. Una Riflessione Fiolosofica," ed. Milena Carrara Pavan (Milan: Jaca Book, 2002, reprinted 2006).

held convictions of the world, many of which we take for granted, are challenged and destabilized. Individuals reckon with—often for the first time—the possibility that their own worldview and ways of living are not the only ones.

The subversive nature of encounter is what makes it *enriching*, for "it allows us to grow, to be transformed; it stimulates us to be more critical, less absolutist, and it widens our scope for tolerance."[8] Nonetheless, Panikkar reminds us that encounter is *difficult*; for the task of being human in relation to others may be simple at a conceptual level but remains incredibly complex and challenging at the practical, everyday level of implementation. In Panikkar's words, "It is easy to talk of dialogue and reconciliation in theory, but to implement it is very hard."[9] It is supposed to be difficult, as are most activities that contribute to well-being, growth, and flourishing, such as physical exercise, dieting, meditating, public speaking, writing, learning a language, reading,

8 Panikkar, "Peace and Interculturality," 190.
9 Panikkar, "Peace and Interculturality," 192.

playing an instrument, honing a skill, serving others, being grateful, managing time, and even budgeting and financial planning. Like all these activities, dialogue across differences is challenging yet healthy, and with practice, it becomes easier, strengthening and building personal and societal resilience.

Bibliography

Abu-Nimer, Mohamed, Anas Alabbadi, and Cynthia Marquez. *Building Bridges*. Kuala Lumpur: World Organization of the Scout Movement and Vienna: International Dialogue Centre, 2018.

Atkinson, Michael. "Paulo Freire." In *Dialogue Theories*, vol. 2, edited by Omer Sener, Frances Sleap, and Paul Weller, 125–38. London: Dialogue Society, 2016.

Bakhtin, Mikhail. *Problems of Dostoevsky's Poetics*. Translated by Caryl Emerson. Minneapolis: University of Minnesota Press, 1984.

Bode, Leticia. "Pruning the News Feed: Unfriending and Unfollowing Political Content on Social Media." *Research and Politics* 3, no. 3 (2016): 1–8. https://doi.org/10.1177/2053168016661873.

Bohm, David. *On Dialogue*. London: Routledge, 2014.

Boghossian, Peter. Interview by Alan Campbell. "Peter Boghossian: How to Have Impossible Conversations." Watching America Podcast, October 16, 2020. https://mediaplayer.whro.org/program/watchingamerica/e/watchingamerica-friday-october-16th-2020.

Boghossian, Peter, and James Lindsay. *How to Have Difficult Conversations*. New York: Hachette, 2019.

Boome, Benjamin. "Managing Differences in Conflict Resolution." In *Conflict Resolution Theory and Practice*, edited by Denis Sandole and Hugo van der Merwe, 97–111. Manchester: Manchester University Press, 1993.

Bryn, Steinar, Inge Edisvåg, and Ingunn Skurdall. *Understanding the Other: Dialogue as a Tool and an Attitude to Life*. Lillehammer: Nansen Fredssenter, 2015.

Buber, Martin. *I and Thou*. Translated by Walter Kaufman. New York: Simon and Schuster, 1970.

Campdepadrós-Cullell, Roger, Miguel Ángel Pulido-Rodríguez, Jesús Marauri, and Sandra Racionero-Plaza. "Interreligious Dialogue Groups Enabling Human Agency." *Religions* 12, no. 3 (2021): 1–15, 189.

Catholic Bishops' Conference of India. "Response of the Church in India to the Present-day Challenges." March 9, 2016. https://www.vatican.va/content/francesco/en/encyclicals/documents/papa-francesco_20201003_enciclica-fratelli-tutti.html#_ftn259.

Cornille, Catherine. "Interreligious Empathy." In *Interreligious Studies: Dispatches from an Emerging Field*, edited by Hans Gustafson, 223–27. Waco, TX: Baylor University Press, 2020.

———. *The Im-Possibility of Interreligious Dialogue*. New York: Crossroad Publishing, 2008.

Credé, Marcus, M. C. Tynan, and P. D. Harms. "Much Ado about Grit: A Meta-Analytic Synthesis of the Grit Literature." *Journal of Personality and Social Psychology* 113, no. 3 (2017): 492–511. https://doi.org/10.1037/pspp0000102.

Eck, Diana L. "Prospects for Pluralism." *Journal of the American Academy of Religion* 75, no. 4 (2007): 743–76. https://doi.org/10.1093/jaarel/lfm061.

Dalai Lama, Fourteenth. "On Compassion." In *Speak Truth to Power: Human Rights Defenders Who Are Changing Our World*, edited by Kerry Kennedy, 35. New York: Umbrage Editions, 2001.

Davis, Daryl. In *When in Doubt*, directed by Travis Brown. Portland, OR, Forthcoming. Trailer videos published online, October 2020. https://www.facebook.com/whenindoubtfilm/videos.

Dialogue Society. "Our Approach." 2019. http://www.dialoguesociety.org/about-us.html.

Duckworth, Angela. *Grit: The Power of Passion and Perseverance*. New York: Scribner / Simon and Schuster, 2016.

Diaman, Jeff. "One-in-Six Americans Have Taken Steps to See Less of Someone on Social Media Due to Religious Content." Pew Research

Center. June 21, 2023. https://www.pewresearch.org/short-reads/2023/06/21/one-in-six-americans-have-taken-steps-to-see-less-of-someone-on-social-media-due-to-religious-content/.

Divali: Festival of Lights Prayer for Hindus. Richmond, VA: International Mission Board of the Southern Baptist Convention, 1990.

Fields, Jennifer R. "Questioning the Promotion of Friendship in Interfaith Dialogue: Interfaith Friendship in Light of the Emphasis on Particularity in Scriptural Reasoning." PhD diss., University of Cambridge, 2020. https://doi.org/10.17863/CAM.51377.

Floyd, Kory, Robert Matheny, Dana R. Dinsmore, Benjamin E. Custer, and Nathan T. Woo. "'If You Disagree, Unfriend Me Now': Exploring the Phenomenon of Invited Unfriending." *American Journal of Applied Psychology* 7, no. 1 (2019): 20–9. https://doi.org/10.12691/ajap-7-1-3.

Francis, Pope. *Fratelli Tutti*. Vatican City: Libreria Editrice Vaticana, 2020.

Gadamer, Hans Georg. *Truth and Method*. 2nd revised ed. Translated in 1989 by Joel Weinsheimer and Donald Marshall. New York: Continuum, 2003.

Grande, Norunn, and Christiane Seehausen, eds. *The Nansen Handbook for Trainers in Dialogue and Conflict Transformation*. Lillehammer: Nansen Fredssenter, 2018.

Green, Paula. *Peacebuilding in Divided Communities*. Amherst, MA: Karuna Center for Peacebuilding, 2012.

Grung, Anne Hege. "Including Gender Perspective in Muslim-Christian Dialogue in Europe and Scandinavia—A Disturbance to Bridge-building or a Contextual Necessity?" In *Mission to the World: Communicating the Gospel in the 21st Century: Essays in Honor of Knud Jørgensen*, edited by Tormod Engelsviken, Ernst Harbakk, Rolv Olsen, and Thor Strandenaes, 289–300. Eugene, OR: Wipf and Stock, 2009.

Gustafson, Hans. *Everyday Wisdom: Interreligious Studies in a Pluralistic World*. Minneapolis: Fortress Press, 2023.

———. "A Primer on Teaching Interreligious Encounter and Undergraduate Course Design." In *Teaching Interreligious Encounters*, edited by Marc A. Pugliese and Alexander Y. Hwang, 136–49. New York: Oxford University Press, 2017.

Gustafson, Hans, ed. *Interreligious Studies: Dispatches from an Emerging Field*. Waco, TX: Baylor University Press, 2020.

Hanh, Thich Nhật. *Being Peace*. Berkeley: Parallax Press, 1987.

Hedges, Paul. *Understanding Religion*. Oakland: University of California Press, 2021.

Jayawickreme, Eranda. "The Power of Intellectual Humility." *Psychology Today*. April 13, 2022. https://www.psychologytoday.com/us/blog/pathways-flourishing/202204/the-power-intellectual-humility.

John Paul II, Pope. *The Attitude of the Church Towards the Followers of Other Religions: Reflections and Orientations on Dialogue and Mission*. Vatican: Pontifical Council for Interreligious Dialogue, 1984.

Karuna Center for Peacebuilding. *Community Dialogue Handbook*, edited by Joanne Lauterjung. Amherst, MA: Karuna Center for Peacebuilding, 2018.

Kaveny, Cathleen. *Prophecy without Contempt*. Cambridge, MA: Harvard University Press, 2016.

King, Sallie B. "Interreligious Dialogue." In *The Oxford Handbook of Religious Diversity*, edited by Chad Meister, 101–14. Oxford: Oxford University Press, 2011.

Lahti, Emilia. "Words Make Our Worlds: Introducing Sisu." *The Creativity Post*, June 5, 2014. https://www.creativitypost.com/psychology/words_make_our_worlds_introducing_sisu.

Lederach, John Paul. *Preparing for Peace: Conflict Transformation across Cultures*. Syracuse, NY: Syracuse University Press, 1995.

Lehmann, Karsten. "Interreligious Dialogue in Context: Towards a Systematic Comparison of IRD-Activities in Europe." *Interdisciplinary Journal for Religion and Transformation in Contemporary Society* 6 (2020): 237–54.

Leirvik, Oddbjørn. "Interreligious Studies: A New Academic Discipline." In *Contested Spaces, Common Ground*, edited by Ulrich Winkler, Lidia

Rodriguez, and Oddbjørn Leirvik, 33–42. Leiden: Brill, 2016.

———. "Philosophies of Interreligious Dialogue: Practice in Search of Theory." *Approaching Religion* 1, no. 1 (2011): 16–24.

Lewis, Jennifer. *Embarking on the Journey of Interreligious Dialogue*. Geneva: The Lutheran World Federation, 2015.

Lindsay, Jenn. "Interfaith Dialogue and Humanization of the Religious Other." *International Journal of Interreligious and Intercultural Studies* 3, no. 2 (2020): 1–24.

Madson, Patricia Ryan. *Improv Wisdom*. New York: Bell Tower, 2005.

McCarthy, Kate. *Interfaith Encounters in America*. New Brunswick, NJ: Rutgers University Press, 2007.

Melnik, Sergey. "Types of Interreligious Dialogue." *Journal of Interreligious Studies* 31 (2020): 54.

Mikva, Rachel S. *Dangerous Religious Ideas*. Boston: Beacon Press, 2020.

———. "Six Issues That Complicate Interreligious Studies and Engagement." In *Interreligious/Interfaith Studies: Defining a New Field*, edited by Eboo Patel, Jennifer Howe Peace, and Noah Silverman, 124–36. Boston: Beacon Press, 2018.

Millis, Diane. *Deepening Engagement*. Woodstock, VT: Skylight Paths, 2015.

Moyaert, Marianne. "Interreligious Dialogue." In *Understanding Interreligious Relations*, edited by

David Cheetham, Douglas Pratt, David Thomas, 193–217. Oxford: Oxford University Press, 2013.

———. "Interreligious Dialogue and the Debate between Universalism and Particularism." *Studies in Interreligious Dialogue* 15, no. 1 (2005): 36–51.

Nansen Peace Center. "Dialogue." Accessed February 9, 2021. https://www.peace.no/dialog/.

Nasr, Seyyed Hossein. *The Need for a Sacred Science*. Albany: SUNY Press, 1993.

Patel, Eboo. "Bridges of Cooperation: Interfaith Action toward Racial Equity." Webinar from College of Saint Benedict, St. Joseph, Minnesota, November 20, 2020. https://www.youtube.com/live/RiiPKKkGo08?feature=shared.

Patel, Eboo, Jennifer Howe Peace, and Noah Silverman, eds. *Interreligious/Interfaith Studies: Defining a New Field*. Boston: Beacon Press, 2018.

Panikkar, Raimon. *The Intrareligious Dialogue*. Revised ed. New York: Paulist Press, 1999.

———. "Peace and Interculturality: A Philosophical Reflection." In *Opera Omnia, Vol. 6: Cultures and Religions in Dialogue, Part One: Pluralism and Interculturality*, edited by Milena Carrara Pavan, 159–212. Maryknoll, NY: Orbis Books, 2018. Originally published as "Pace e Interculturalitá. Una Riflessione Filosofica," edited by Milena Carrara Pavan. Milan: Jaca Book, 2002, reprinted 2006.

———. "Some Notes on Syncretism and Eclecticism: Related to the Growth of Human Consciousness."

In *Opera Omnia, Vol. 6: Cultures and Religions in Dialogue, Part One: Pluralism and Interculturality*, edited by Milena Carrara Pavan, 94–102. Maryknoll, NY: Orbis Books, 2018. Originally published in *Religious Syncretism in Antiquity: Essays in Conversation with Geo Widengren*, edited by B. A. Pearson, 47–62. Missoula, MT: Scholars Press, 1975.

———. "Toward a Theory of Intercultural and Interreligious Liberation." In *Opera Omnia, Vol. 6: Cultures and Religions in Dialogue, Part One: Pluralism and Interculturality*, edited by Milena Carrara Pavan, 140–43. Maryknoll, NY: Orbis Books, 2018. Originally published as "Hacia una Teología de la Liberación." In *Interculturalidad, Diálogo y Liberación*, edited by H. Küng, J. J. Tamayo-Acosta, and R. Forneet-Betancourt, 61–68. Pamplona: Verbo Divino, 2005.

Pluralism Project. "What Is Pluralism?" Accessed April 1, 2021. https://pluralism.org/about.

Pontifical Council for Inter-religious Dialogue. *Dialogue and Proclamation: Reflection and Orientations on Interreligious Dialogue and the Proclamation of the Gospel of Jesus Christ*. Vatican: Pontifical Council for Interreligious Dialogue, 1991.

Pugliese, Marc A., and Alexander Y. Hwang, eds. *Teaching Interreligious Encounter*. New York: Oxford University Press, 2017.

Ramsbotham, Oliver. "Hans-Georg Gadamer." In *Dialogue Theories*, vol. 2, edited by Omer Sener,

Frances Sleap, and Paul Weller, 139–56. London: Dialogue Society, 2016.

Rosenberg, Marshall B. *Nonviolent Communication: A Language of Life*. 3rd ed. Encinitas, CA: Puddle Dancer Press, 2015.

Schaffner, Anna Katharina. *The Art of Self-Improvement*. New Haven, CT: Yale University Press, 2021.

Schirch, Lisa, and David Campt. *The Little Book of Dialogue for Difficult Subjects: A Practical, Hands-On Guide*. Intercourse, PA: Good Books, 2007.

Sener, Omer, Frances Sleap, and Paul Weller, eds. *Dialogue Theories*, vol. 2. London: Dialogue Society, 2016.

Shallwani, Pervaiz. "Life Lessons from the NYPD's Top Hostage Negotiator." *Wall Street Journal*, August 29, 2015. https://www.wsj.com/articles/life-lessons-from-the-nypds-top-hostage-negotiator-1440726792.

Sharma, Arvind. "The Meaning and Goals of Interreligious Dialogue." *Journal of Dharma* 8, no. 3 (1983): 225–47.

Sharpe, Eric J. "The Goals of Inter-Religious Dialogue." In *Truth and Dialogue in World Religions*, edited by John Hick, 77–95. Philadelphia: Westminster Press, 1974.

Shires, Jeff. "Mikhail Bakhtin." In *Dialogue Theories*, vol. 2, edited by Omer Sener, Frances Sleap, and Paul Weller, 29–42. London: Dialogue Society, 2016.

Sleap, Frances, and Omer Sener. "Introduction." In *Dialogue Theories*, edited by Paul Weller, 15–20. London: Dialogue Society, 2013.

Smith, Rachel Hostetter, ed. *Between Shadow and the Light*. Grand Rapids, MI: Calvin College, 2014.

Smith, Tovia. "'Dude, I'm Done': When Politics Tears Families and Friendships Apart." NPR.org. October 27, 2020. Heard on *All Things Considered*. https://www.npr.org/2020/10/27/928209548/dude-im-done-when-politics-tears-families-and-friendships-apart.

Svare, Helge, in cooperation with the Council for Religious and Life Stance Communities. "Explanation of the Dialogue Poster." The Council for Religious and Life Stance Communities, Oslo, 2017.

Stringer, Martin D. "Lived Religion and Difficult Conversations." Birmingham Conversations of the Faith, Neighbors, Changemakers Collaboration, Birmingham, 2015.

Swidler, Leonard. *Dialogue for Interreligious Understanding*. New York: Palgrave Macmillan, 2014.

Taylor, Richard W. "The Meaning of Dialogue." In *Inter-religious Dialogue*, edited by Herbert Jai Singh, 55–64. Bangalore: The Christian Institute for the Study of Religion and Society, 1967.

Tulku, Chagdud, compiled and edited by Lama Shenpen Drolma. *Change of Heart: The Bodhisattva Peace Training of Chagdud Tulku*. Junction City, CA: Padma Publishing, 2003.

United States Office of the Surgeon General. "Our Epidemic of Loneliness and Isolation: The Surgeon General's Advisory on the Healing Effects of Social Connection and Community." 2023. https://www.hhs.gov/sites/default/files/surgeon-general-social-connection-advisory.pdf.

Unno, Mark. "Buddhist-Christian Dialogue: Mystery of the Naked Heart." *Buddhist-Christian Studies* 40 (2020): 307–26.

Varnon-Hughes, Stephanie. *Interfaith Grit: How Uncertainty Will Save Us*. Eugene, OR: Wipf and Stock, 2018.

Vrudny, Kimberly. "Artists as Prophets and Visionaries: An Ubuntu-Inspired Renewal of Christianity." In *Between Shadow and the Light*, edited by Rachel Hostetter Smith, 31–40. Grand Rapids, MI: Calvin College, 2014.

Webster, R. Scott. "An Existential Framework of Spirituality." *International Journal of Children's Spirituality* 9, no. 1 (2004): 7–19.

Whitehead, Alfred North. *Process and Reality*. Corrected ed., edited by David Ray Griffin and Donald W. Sherburne. New York: Free Press, 1978.

Wilshere, Andrew. "Emmanuel Levinas." In *Dialogue Theories*, vol. 2, edited by Omer Sener, Frances Sleap, and Paul Weller, 189–204. London: Dialogue Society, 2016.

Young, Neil, and Crazy Horse. "Falling from Above." Track 1 on *Greendale*. Warner Bros., 2003, compact disc.

Index